LANGUAGE AND LITERACY SERIES

Dorothy S. Strickland, FOUNDING EDITOR
Donna E. Alvermann and María Paula Ghiso, SERIES EDITORS
ADVISORY BOARD: Richard Allington, Kathryn Au, Bernice Cullinan, Colette Daiute,
Anne Haas Dyson, Carole Edelsky, Mary Juzwik, Susan Lytle, Django Paris, Timothy Shanahan

Writing Instruction for Success in College
and in the Workplace
CHARLES A. MACARTHUR & ZOI A. PHILIPPAKOS

Black Immigrant Literacies: Intersections of Race,
Language, and Culture in the Classroom
PATRIANN SMITH

Teens Choosing to Read: Fostering Social,
Emotional, and Intellectual Growth Through Books
GAY IVEY & PETER JOHNSTON

Critical Encounters in Secondary English:
Teaching Literary Theory to Adolescents,
4th Edition
DEBORAH APPLEMAN

Reading With Purpose: Selecting and Using
Children's Literature for Inquiry and Engagement
ERIKA THULIN DAWES, KATIE EGAN CUNNINGHAM,
GRACE ENRIQUEZ, & MARY ANN CAPPIELLO

Core Practices for Teaching Multilingual Students:
Humanizing Pedagogies for Equity
MEGAN MADIGAN PEERCY, JOHANNA M. TIGERT, &
DAISY E. FREDRICKS

Bringing Sports Culture to the English Classroom:
An Interest-Driven Approach to Literacy
Instruction
LUKE RODESILER

Culturally Sustaining Literacy Pedagogies:
Honoring Students' Heritages, Literacies, and
Languages
SUSAN CHAMBERS CANTRELL, DORIS WALKER-DALHOUSE,
& ALTHIER M. LAZAR, EDS.

Curating a Literacy Life:
Student-Centered Learning With Digital Media
WILLIAM KIST

Understanding the Transnational Lives and
Literacies of Immigrant Children
JUNGMIN KWON

The Administration and Supervision of Literacy
Programs, 6th Edition
SHELLEY B. WEPNER & DIANA J. QUATROCHE, EDS.

Writing the School House Blues: Literacy, Equity,
and Belonging in a Child's Early Schooling
ANNE HAAS DYSON

Playing With Language: Improving Elementary
Reading Through Metalinguistic Awareness
MARCY ZIPKE

Restorative Literacies:
Creating a Community of Care in Schools
DEBORAH L. WOLTER

Compose Our World: Project-Based Learning in
Secondary English Language Arts
ALISON G. BOARDMAN, ANTERO GARCIA, BRIDGET
DALTON, & JOSEPH L. POLMAN

Digitally Supported Disciplinary Literacy for
Diverse K–5 Classrooms
JAMIE COLWELL, AMY HUTCHISON,
& LINDSAY WOODWARD

The Reading Turn-Around with Emergent
Bilinguals: A Five-Part Framework for Powerful
Teaching and Learning (Grades K-6)
AMANDA CLAUDIA WAGER, LANE W. CLARKE,
& GRACE ENRIQUEZ

Race, Justice, and Activism in Literacy Instruction
VALERIE KINLOCH, TANJA BURKHARD,
& CARLOTTA PENN, EDS.

Letting Go of Literary Whiteness:
Antiracist Literature Instruction for White Students
CARLIN BORSHEIM-BLACK
& SOPHIA TATIANA SARIGIANIDES

The Vulnerable Heart of Literacy:
Centering Trauma as Powerful Pedagogy
ELIZABETH DUTRO

Amplifying the Curriculum: Designing Quality
Learning Opportunities for English Learners
AÍDA WALQUI & GEORGE C. BUNCH, EDS.

Arts Integration in Diverse K–5 Classrooms:
Cultivating Literacy Skills and Conceptual
Understanding
LIANE BROUILLETTE

Translanguaging for Emergent Bilinguals: Inclusive
Teaching in the Linguistically Diverse Classroom
DANLING FU, XENIA HADJIOANNOU, & XIAODI ZHOU

Before Words: Wordless Picture Books and the
Development of Reading in Young Children
JUDITH T. LYSAKER

Seeing the Spectrum: Teaching English Language
Arts to Adolescents with Autism
ROBERT ROZEMA

A Think-Aloud Approach to Writing Assessment:
Analyzing Process and Product with Adolescent
Writers
SARAH W. BECK

"We've Been Doing It Your Way Long Enough":
Choosing the Culturally Relevant Classroom
JANICE BAINES, CARMEN TISDALE, & SUSI LONG

Summer Reading: Closing the Rich/Poor
Reading Achievement Gap, 2nd Edition
RICHARD L. ALLINGTON & ANNE MCGILL-FRANZEN, EDS.

Educating for Empathy:
Literacy Learning and Civic Engagement
NICOLE MIRRA

Preparing English Learners for College and Career:
Lessons from Successful High Schools
MARÍA SANTOS ET AL.

Reading the Rainbow: LGBTQ-Inclusive Literacy
Instruction in the Elementary Classroom
CAITLIN L. RYAN & JILL M. HERMANN-WILMARTH

continued

For volumes in the NCRLL Collection (edited by JoBeth Allen and Donna E. Alvermann) and the Practitioners Bookshelf Series (edited by Celia Genishi and Donna E. Alvermann), as well as other titles in this series, please visit www.tcpress.com

Language and Literacy Series, *continued*

Educating Emergent Bilinguals, 2nd Ed.
OFELIA GARCÍA & JO ANNE KLEIFGEN

Social Justice Literacies in the English Classroom
ASHLEY S. BOYD

Remixing Multiliteracies
FRANK SERAFINI & ELISABETH GEE, EDS.

Culturally Sustaining Pedagogies
DJANGO PARIS & H. SAMY ALIM, EDS.

Choice and Agency in the Writing Workshop
FRED L. HAMEL

Assessing Writing, Teaching Writers
MARY ANN SMITH & SHERRY SEALE SWAIN

The Teacher-Writer
CHRISTINE M. DAWSON

Every Young Child a Reader
SHARAN A. GIBSON & BARBARA MOSS

"You Gotta BE the Book," 3rd Ed.
JEFFREY D. WILHELM

Personal Narrative, Revised
BRONWYN CLARE LAMAY

Inclusive Literacy Teachings
LORI HELMAN ET AL.

The Vocabulary Book, 2nd Ed.
MICHAEL F. GRAVES

Reading, Writing, and Talk
MARIANA SOUTO-MANNING & JESSICA MARTELL

Go Be a Writer!
CANDACE R. KUBY & TARA GUTSHALL RUCKER

Partnering with Immigrant Communities
GERALD CAMPANO ET AL.

Teaching Outside the Box but Inside the Standards
BOB FECHO ET AL., EDS.

Literacy Leadership in Changing Schools
SHELLEY B. WEPNER ET AL.

Literacy Theory as Practice
LARA J. HANDSFIELD

Literacy and History in Action
THOMAS M. MCCANN ET AL.

Pose, Wobble, Flow
ANTERO GARCIA & CINDY O'DONNELL-ALLEN

Newsworthy
ED MADISON

Engaging Writers with Multigenre Research Projects
NANCY MACK

Teaching Transnational Youth
ALLISON SKERRETT

Uncommonly Good Ideas
SANDRA MURPHY & MARY ANN SMITH

The One-on-One Reading and Writing Conference
JENNIFER BERNE & SOPHIE C. DEGENER

Transforming Talk into Text
THOMAS M. MCCANN

Educating Literacy Teachers Online
LANE W. CLARKE & SUSAN WATTS-TAFFEE

WHAM! Teaching with Graphic Novels Across the Curriculum
WILLIAM G. BROZO ET AL.

Critical Literacy in the Early Childhood Classroom
CANDACE R. KUBY

Inspiring Dialogue
MARY M. JUZWIK ET AL.

Reading the Visual
FRANK SERAFINI

ReWRITING the Basics
ANNE HAAS DYSON

Writing Instruction That Works
ARTHUR N. APPLEBEE ET AL.

Literacy Playshop
KAREN E. WOHLWEND

Critical Media Pedagogy
ERNEST MORRELL ET AL.

A Search Past Silence
DAVID E. KIRKLAND

The ELL Writer
CHRISTINA ORTMEIER-HOOPER

Reading in a Participatory Culture
HENRY JENKINS ET AL., EDS.

Teaching Vocabulary to English Language Learners
MICHAEL F. GRAVES ET AL.

Bridging Literacy and Equity
ALTHIER M. LAZAR ET AL.

Reading Time
CATHERINE COMPTON-LILLY

Interrupting Hate
MOLLIE V. BLACKBURN

Playing Their Way into Literacies
KAREN E. WOHLWEND

Teaching Literacy for Love and Wisdom
JEFFREY D. WILHELM & BRUCE NOVAK

Urban Literacies
VALERIE KINLOCH, ED.

Bedtime Stories and Book Reports
CATHERINE COMPTON-LILLY & STUART GREENE, EDS.

Envisioning Knowledge
JUDITH A. LANGER

Envisioning Literature, 2nd Ed.
JUDITH A. LANGER

Artifactual Literacies
KATE PAHL & JENNIFER ROWSELL

Change Is Gonna Come
PATRICIA A. EDWARDS ET AL.

Harlem on Our Minds
VALERIE KINLOCH

Children, Language, and Literacy
CELIA GENISHI & ANNE HAAS DYSON

Children's Language
JUDITH WELLS LINDFORS

Storytime
LAWRENCE R. SIPE

Writing Instruction for Success in College and in the Workplace

Charles A. MacArthur
Zoi A. Philippakos

Foreword by Dolores Perin

Teachers College Press
TEACHERS COLLEGE | COLUMBIA UNIVERSITY
NEW YORK AND LONDON

Published by Teachers College Press,® 1234 Amsterdam Avenue, New York, NY 10027

Copyright © 2023 by Teachers College, Columbia University

Front cover design by Edwin Kuo. Image by Hulinska Yevheniia / Shutterstock.

All rights reserved. No part of this publication may be reproduced or transmitted in any form or by any means, electronic or mechanical, including photocopy, or any information storage and retrieval system, without permission from the publisher. For reprint permission and other subsidiary rights requests, please contact Teachers College Press, Rights Dept.: tcpressrights@tc.columbia.edu

The research reported here was supported by the Institute of Education Sciences, U.S. Department of Education, through Grant R305A160242 to University of Delaware, An Efficacy Trial of a Postsecondary Strategic Writing Intervention, PI Charles MacArthur. The opinions expressed are those of the authors and do not represent views of the Institute or the U.S. Department of Education. We are not aware of any conflicts of interest.

Library of Congress Cataloging-in-Publication Data

Names: MacArthur, Charles A., author. | Philippakos, Zoi A., author.
Title: Writing instruction for success in college and in the workplace / Charles A. MacArthur and Zoi A. Philippakos ; foreword by Dolores Perin.
Description: New York, NY : Teachers College Press, 2024. | Series: Language and literacy series | Includes bibliographical references and index. | Summary: "This book describes an innovative, evidence-based method for teaching developmental writing. The goal is to help students become independent learners who can apply strategies to future college courses and the workplace"—Provided by publisher.
Identifiers: LCCN 2023031679 (print) | LCCN 2023031680 (ebook) | ISBN 9780807768808 (paperback) | ISBN 9780807768815 (hardcover) | ISBN 9780807781951 (ebook)
Subjects: LCSH: Composition (Language arts)—Study and teaching (Secondary) | English language—Composition and exercises—Study and teaching (Secondary)
Classification: LCC LB1631 .M25 2024 (print) | LCC LB1631 (ebook) | DDC 808/.0420712—dc23/eng/20230814
LC record available at https://lccn.loc.gov/2023031679
LC ebook record available at https://lccn.loc.gov/2023031680

ISBN 978-0-8077-6880-8 (paper)
ISBN 978-0-8077-6881-5 (hardcover)
ISBN 978-0-8077-8195-1 (ebook)

Printed on acid-free paper
Manufactured in the United States of America

Contents

Foreword *Dolores Perin* ix

Preface xi
    Development of the Supporting Strategic Writers Program xii
    Organization of Our Book xiii
    Conclusion xiv

PART I. INTRODUCTION TO SUPPORTING STRATEGIC WRITERS

1. **Addressing Challenges in Postsecondary Education: The Genesis of Supporting Strategic Writers and Research Findings** 3
    Developmental Writing 4
    College Expectations 5
    Supporting Strategic Writers Project 6
    Research on Supporting Strategic Writers 7
    Conclusion 9

2. **Core Instructional Components of Supporting Strategic Writers** 11
    Core Principles of Strategy Instruction 12
    Writing Strategies 13
    Metacognition and Motivation 20
    Pedagogical Methods 22
    Instructional Sequence: A Strategy for Teaching Strategies 24
    Conclusion 26

PART II. SSW WRITING STRATEGIES

3. Planning and Drafting for Argumentative Writing Without Sources — 31
- Explanation and Modeling of the Strategy — 32
- Collaborative Practice — 45
- Guided Practice — 46
- Conclusion — 47

4. Evaluating and Revising for Argumentative Writing Without Sources — 49
- Strategies for Evaluation and Revision — 49
- Introduction to a New Genre — 50
- Preparation for Peer Review — 50
- Peer Review and Revision — 55
- Reflection — 55
- Conclusion — 56

5. Challenges of Writing Using Sources; Summary-Response — 59
- SSW Strategies for Writing Using Sources — 60
- Instruction Following the Strategy for Teaching Strategies — 61
- Connecting Summary-Response to Writing Essays With Sources — 74
- Conclusion — 74

6. Integrating Ideas From Sources in an Essay — 77
- Sequence of Assignments — 77
- Introduction to Writing Using Sources — 78
- Integrate Ideas From Sources With Your Own Ideas — 78
- Plan Your Essay: Organize Ideas With the Argument Go — 82
- Draft the Essay — 83
- Further Assignments — 84
- Selecting Sources — 85
- Conclusion — 86

PART III. A LOOK TO THE FUTURE

7. Addressing Challenges in Implementation and Problem-Solving — 91
  Challenges With the Use of Cognitive Strategies — 91
  Institutional Organizational Structures — 97
  End of Semester Reflection — 98
  Conclusion — 98

8. Extending the Strategies to Other Genres and Other Courses — 101
  Adapting Strategies to Genres Across Courses — 101
  Examples of Applying the SSW Strategies in Other Courses — 102
  Concluding Thoughts — 105

References — 107

Index — 115

About the Authors — 119

Foreword

It would be hard to find anyone who would disagree with the contention that writing is an extremely important activity in education, in personal life, in civic participation, and in the economy as a whole. Yet I don't think I am exaggerating when I say that only a tiny minority of people find it easy to write, and even fewer would call themselves "good writers." As writing becomes an increasingly important mode of communication in our society, it has become a matter of urgency to teach writing skills in an effective way. This is especially true for the large number of adults who have high aspirations for educational and economic advancement but are held back by underdeveloped writing skills. There have been many approaches to teaching writing, but few methods have been shown to be effective through sound research.

At this critical juncture, we have a book that presents a far-reaching approach to teaching writing to academically underprepared adults, supported by years of careful research. I was delighted to learn that the authors, Charles MacArthur and Zoi Philippakos, had written a book that would point the way to effective writing instruction for the many college instructors who are committed to helping their students succeed in education and beyond. I have known the authors for many years and have followed their work with great interest. I myself have conducted studies of the writing of adults who need assistance with writing skills and am convinced, based on the data from MacArthur and Philippakos's studies, that their approach is the gold standard of writing instruction for this population.

At the heart of their method, "Supporting Strategic Writers," is, as the name suggests, writing *strategy*. There is an important educational principle at the root of strategy instruction: procedural knowledge, otherwise known as teaching *how* to do something. How can we be good at a difficult skill without being shown how it's done? Through this book, instructors will learn how to show their students how to write, step by step. Further, students in turn will learn steps for expressing information and their thoughts in a meaningful and coherent way.

So this book provides procedural knowledge for teachers and students alike. Both teachers and students are often immensely relieved when they are shown how to do something they find difficult. Any instructor who teaches writing, or indeed merely expects good writing from students (and despairs when receiving poorly written work) can breathe more easily when they are shown how to help their students with this challenging skill. MacArthur and Philippakos provide expert guidance on this journey.

I see at least four reasons why this book is especially important. *First*, the Supporting Strategic Writers approach is comprehensive in covering step-by-step strategies for planning, drafting, revising, and editing writing, as well as the metacognitive dimensions that surround writing, including learner self-regulation, motivation, and self-efficacy. The authors also provide practical supports for these steps, such as mnemonics that guide the writing process, as well as self-monitoring charts, graphic organizers, and other physical displays. Key to the SSW approach, and often missing from other approaches to teaching writing, is the modeling process, where the instructor actually shows students how to write to a specific prompt. Based on my experience with students who need help with writing, I can say that modeling by teachers is a crucial aspect of writing instruction—this book explains how modeling each step of the writing process can be performed effectively. At the same time, based on their research, the authors point out that there are times when modeling would not be helpful; rather, student collaborative practice would be more appropriate.

Second, the authors show how the SSW approach can be used to teach a variety of writing genres, including argumentative writing, descriptive writing, compare-contrast and cause-and-effect writing, written summarization, and personal narrative. *Third*, all aspects of the SSW approach are supported by rigorous research conducted over many years both by the authors and by earlier researchers who produced classic studies. Further, the authors have field-tested their method in college classrooms with good results. *Fourth*, the book is written in a direct and clear style (demonstrating good writing practice!) that makes it immediately accessible to busy educators and researchers alike.

I cannot say enough good things about this book, and I think it represents a milestone not only in the teaching method it presents but in the translation of the highest quality research into a usable text that both informs teaching practice and also provides a foundation for future research that aims at understanding the writing of adults who are academically underprepared for the writing demands of higher education.

—Dolores Perin
Professor Emerita, Psychology and Education
Teachers College, Columbia University

Preface

Many first-year college students are required to take noncredit developmental courses in writing, but only a minority complete these courses and pass a first-year composition (FYC) course. This problem is currently being addressed by colleges with several structural reforms: changing placement procedures, offering integrated reading and writing courses in place of separate developmental reading and writing courses, and providing co-requisite courses and compressed courses to help students complete FYC in the first year of college. However, little research has focused on instructional methods for teaching writing in the classroom. Since 2010, with funding from the U.S. Department of Education, our Supporting Strategic Writers Project has been working collaboratively with community college faculty to develop instructional approaches for writing and reading and then to test these approaches in rigorous experimental studies. Our research over 10 years has consistently found strong positive effects on writing quality and motivation.

Our research has been conducted in developmental writing and integrated reading/writing courses, but the instructional approaches have been designed to align with the requirements of first-year composition and the writing demands of other college courses. The goals of the Supporting Strategic Writers (SSW) program are that students will develop knowledge of academic writing genres; strategies for critical reading, planning, and revising; and the motivational beliefs that support continued critical reading and writing in the future (CWPA, 2011). Thus, the instructional approaches are adaptable to co-requisite courses and first-year composition. Many of the instructors who worked with us in the research studies have, in fact, used our curriculum in other writing courses.

In this program, students learn strategies for critical reading, planning, drafting, and revising along with metacognitive self-regulation strategies that help students take control of the writing process and their learning. The strategies are based on the purposes and organizational elements of common types of writing, or genres. These elements are reflected in the design of graphic organizers used during planning and in the content of evaluation rubrics for revising. For planning, students learn to analyze tasks for topic, audience, and purpose; to generate ideas through brainstorming, and to organize their ideas using graphic organizers based on text structures.

For critical reading of sources, students learn to look for the genre elements in taking notes on main ideas. For revising, students learn to evaluate their papers using criteria based on the text elements (e.g., Is my position stated clearly?). The program places substantial emphasis on learning self-evaluation; therefore, the revising instruction includes training and practice in peer review and self-evaluation.

In addition to specific writing strategies, students learn strategies for metacognitive self-regulation. The curriculum includes an overall strategy, Strategies for Academic Success, which includes goal setting, task management, monitoring of progress, and reflection. The Strategies for Academic Success guide students to consider their long-term goals as well as to set specific goals for particular writing tasks. Finally, after the writing task is completed, evaluated, and revised, students reflect on their writing and whether the writing strategies were helpful, and how they might modify them in the future. These reflections lead to new goals for writing and strategy use for the next writing task. Through this program, students develop as writers who can independently write using strategies across contexts and settings.

DEVELOPMENT OF THE SUPPORTING STRATEGIC WRITERS PROGRAM

This research program was initially motivated by our awareness of the problems of developmental writing—the large numbers of students, the disappointing outcomes in terms of college success, and the very limited research on instruction. Our reading of the literature on basic writing led us to conclude that although there was a wealth of publications on instructional practices and on rhetorical approaches, the research on the effects of instructional approaches on student writing outcomes was slim to nonexistent. Thus, in 2010, we began a research collaboration with colleagues at local community colleges to conduct design research using mixed qualitative and quantitative methods. At the time, community colleges were offering separate developmental courses in reading and writing. Thus, our first development work focused on writing without the use of sources. We were also aware of the problems of writing anxiety and lack of confidence, so we also set out to evaluate the impact of instruction on motivation. We and our collaborators were excited to find positive effects on writing quality and motivation, and our interviews with students showed their greater understanding of the value of planning and peer reviewing and their growing confidence and purpose in their writing.

After two experimental studies confirmed the positive effects of the SSW program on writing quality and motivation, we turned our efforts to extending the curriculum to include writing using sources. For success in first-year composition and college courses, students need to be able to use sources in their writing. We conducted design research with the college partners who had already participated in our research and then conducted another experimental study that found positive effects. The research studies mentioned here are summarized in Chapter 1.

We continue to work to improve the instructional program with the colleagues and colleges who participated in the studies.

ORGANIZATION OF OUR BOOK

The book is organized into three sections and eight chapters. Chapter 1, *Addressing Challenges in Postsecondary Education: The Genesis of Supporting Strategic Writers and Research Findings*, reviews the knowledge, strategies, and skills that postsecondary writers need for academic writing, and analyzes the literacy challenges of postsecondary learners. The chapter also summarizes the research on SSW, including the design research to develop and refine the instruction and the experimental studies to test and validate the program.

Chapter 2, *Core Instructional Components of Supporting Strategic Writers*, discusses the key principles of strategy instruction and how they are applied in SSW. First, the writing strategies are explained. Students learn to use knowledge about the purpose and form of different genres of writing to plan and revise, as well as to support reading of sources. Second, students learn metacognitive strategies for goal setting, task management, progress monitoring, and reflection. These strategies are essential to help students feel in control of the writing process, adapt strategies to new situations, and take responsibility for their own learning. Third, pedagogical methods are critical, including think-aloud modeling, collaborative practice, and discussions of how to apply the strategies in other courses.

Chapter 3, *Planning and Drafting for Argumentative Writing Without Sources*, explains the writing strategies in more detail, focusing on the argument, which is critical to college success. The planning strategies are based on the purposes and organization of genres. Students learn strategies that include rhetorical task analysis, brainstorming, and organization. The strategies and the instructional methods are explained with examples. Ways to support drafting through use of sentence frames and collaborative writing are also explained.

Chapter 4, *Evaluating and Revising for Argumentative Writing Without Sources*, explains the strategies for revision and the procedures for teaching them. Learning to self-evaluate one's writing is critical to growth as a writer. Students learn to use genre-specific rubrics for peer review and self-evaluation. Our own research shows that "giving feedback" as part of peer review is instrumental in improving one's own writing, because it helps students learn evaluation criteria, which will transfer to self-evaluation. The process of reviewing and evaluating is explained with an emphasis on the processes and value of peer review. Examples of evaluative comments are provided as samples.

Chapter 5, *Challenges of Writing Using Sources; Summary-Response*, discusses the demands of writing with sources and explains how writing summary-response essays on single sources can provide a transition to essays with sources. Writing from sources requires students to read critically to understand authors' ideas, and then synthesize ideas across sources to incorporate them into the students' own papers. The strategies for critical reading and notetaking, and for using those notes to write summary-response essays are explained. The critical reading strategy uses knowledge about the purposes and organization of genres to guide comprehension and critical evaluation of sources. Summary-response papers are common in college courses, and they offer a path to improving comprehension and note-taking. The strategies and instructional procedures are explained with specific examples.

Chapter 6, *Integrating Ideas from Sources in an Essay*, continues the strategies for writing with sources, focusing on how to integrate, or synthesize, information across sources to write a paper. After gathering information from sources, writers must engage in a process of comparing and integrating ideas from multiple sources. Students return to the planning and revising strategies with a new focus on integration of sources. The process will be explained for readers.

Chapter 7, *Addressing Challenges in Implementation and Problem-Solving*, draws on our extensive experience working with instructors to solve problems about classroom implementation. We discuss common questions and challenges and offer advice about avoiding problems and solving them when they occur.

Chapter 8, *Extending the Strategies to Other Genres and Other Courses*, explains how the SSW approach has been applied beyond our rigorous research in developmental writing and integrated reading and writing courses. We continued to collaborate with instructors who participated in the studies as they applied the SSW approach in first-year composition, co-requisite courses, first-year seminars, summer programs, and courses in other content areas. In this chapter, we also discuss potential applications of strategy instruction in technical writing courses to prepare students for workplace writing.

CONCLUSION

We hope you find this book helpful in your instruction. We would like to thank the teachers who worked with us and who continue to work with us as professional developers and implementers of this approach. We were fortunate to work with knowledgeable and creative individuals who care for their students and their own learning. It was a joy and inspiration working with them.

Further, we are grateful for the college students who worked with us. We have wonderful memories of working with students and celebrating their growth and learning. We worked with students who had been disappointed by the educational system, and we saw them grow in confidence and writing skill. Students gave us their perspectives on how the strategies worked, and we learned from them. We heard from some who used the instructional approaches in other classrooms. We also heard their challenges and struggles after not receiving adequate preparation for writing in high school. We were inspired by them and wish them the best in their next career steps.

We would also like to thank those who consulted with us and shared their recommendations about measures, assessments, procedures, and revisions. We thank our research consultants Dolores Perin and Steve Graham. We also thank the college instructors who continued to work with us as consultants after participating in the research: Michelle Blake, Katherine Cottle, Kim Donnelly, Caitlin Gallagher, Marie Nester, and Eric Nefferdorf. We also acknowledge the informal consultants who joined our sessions at the Literacy Research Association (LRA), the American Association of Colleges for Teacher Education (AACTE), the National Organization for Student Success (NOSS), the Conference on College Composition and Communication (CCCC), the College English Association (CEA), and many others.

Further, we would like to thank the Institute of Education Sciences (IES) and our program officer, Meredith Larson, who encouraged and supported us across all stages of implementation.

Finally, we want to thank Teachers College Press who offered a home to this work and gave us the opportunity to share our research and materials with all of you, our readers.

Writing Instruction for Success in College and in the Workplace

Part I

INTRODUCTION TO SUPPORTING STRATEGIC WRITERS

Part 1

CHAPTER 1

Addressing Challenges in Postsecondary Education
The Genesis of Supporting Strategic Writers and Research Findings

> I want to become a better writer! I want to be able to express myself through writing. I want to make my college experience easier by gaining a better understanding of how to manage writing skill to meet deadlines. I also want to practice writing strategies until they become second nature. My fear of writing is based in ignorance and embarrassment because of what I lack as a writer. I want better for myself.
>
> —reflection written by a student participant

College writing can be demanding, and many high school graduates are not adequately prepared for the challenge. The transition from the limited writing instruction offered in most high schools to the expectations for independent writing in college is challenging for many students. As the student shared at the opening of this chapter, there is fear of writing as well as embarrassment that can affect the confidence of writers and their efforts. Similarly, adults who pursue a college degree some years after high school may find academic writing challenging and disheartening. Students who enter college without adequate preparation in writing, regardless of whether or not they were recent high school graduates, want to do better. College faculty and researchers need to work together to address this problem and support students in their goals to have a better quality of life.

A large study by Applebee and Langer (2011), which included a national survey of 1,520 secondary teachers and class observations and interviews with over 200 secondary teachers at schools with reputations for excellent writing instruction, found relatively little time devoted to writing instruction and practice even in English classrooms and almost none in science and social studies; teachers explained that the limited writing was due to the time required to give feedback. The consequences are evident in results from the National Assessment of Education Progress (NAEP) in writing (National Center for Education Statistics, 2012), which found that only 27% of grade-12 students performed at or above the proficient level. At the same time, 60% to 70% of high school students go to college (Bureau of Labor Statistics, 2022).

The goal of our research over the past decade has been to support instructors in teaching students who find writing at the college level extremely demanding. In this chapter, we address the challenges that writing poses to postsecondary students and their instructors and share the findings from our research, which has led to the development and validation of a writing program for postsecondary students.

DEVELOPMENTAL WRITING

Considering the NAEP writing results, it is not surprising that in the United States about a quarter to a third of new community college students are required to take noncredit remedial courses, or developmental courses, in writing or reading (Bailey et al., 2010; Chen, 2016). Even at 4-year public colleges, 11% of students take developmental writing. Many colleges offer two levels of developmental writing, so some students need to take two developmental courses before enrolling in first-year composition (FYC). Developmental courses offer a second chance at college success for students who need extra support. Students who complete the developmental courses and go on to take FYC generally do as well in college as nondevelopmental students (Bailey et al., 2010; Chen, 2016). However, most students drop out before completing the required developmental courses. Using a large set of data from the Achieving the Dream project, Bailey and colleagues (2010) found that only 37% of students placed in developmental reading ever passed a related credit course. A study at a community college with high minority enrollment (Nastal-Dema, 2019) found that only 12% of students who took developmental writing ever passed FYC. Overall, students who are referred to developmental education are less likely to graduate (Bailey et al., 2010; Chen, 2016).

In response to the problems in developmental education, researchers have studied structural changes in how developmental education is organized (MacArthur, 2023). One change is to use multiple measures, including high school grade-point average (GPA), for placement, which has resulted in fewer students being placed in developmental education, and, overall, more students passing FYC in the first year of college (Barnett et al., 2020). Another structural change is to combine two developmental courses into a single course to help students complete the requirements sooner. Studies that combined two levels of developmental writing (Hodara & Jaggars, 2014) or integrated reading and writing into a single developmental course (Edgecombe et al., 2014) have found positive effects on successfully completing FYC. Another innovation is co-requisite courses, which enroll students simultaneously in FYC and a developmental support course; research (Cho et al., 2012) has found positive effects on completing FYC successfully.

In contrast to the amount of research on structural changes, little systematic research has focused on improving instructional methods. Basic writing is an active field of scholarship, and many resources are available with recommendations for instruction in developmental reading and writing (e.g., Adams, 2019; Flippo & Bean, 2018). However, few studies have investigated the effects of instructional approaches on students' writing performance and quality of writing. A review of research on instruction in developmental writing (Perin & Holschuh, 2019) included over 30 studies, but most were descriptive reports of instructional practices, sometimes including a pretest and posttest. The only experimental study included in that review other than our research was a study by Perin (2013) on summary writing. The need for more research on instructional approaches led to our research program to examine *what works* for students to improve writing performance and motivation.

COLLEGE EXPECTATIONS

The Council of Writing Program Administrators (CWPA, 2014) created a set of goals or outcomes for first-year composition programs. The writing outcomes address rhetorical knowledge; critical thinking, reading, and composing; composing processes or strategies; and knowledge of conventions. Rhetorical knowledge includes the ability to analyze contexts, audiences, and purposes and apply that analysis in critical reading and writing. It includes understanding the genres used in varied contexts including academic disciplines. Critical thinking is defined to include analysis, interpretation, evaluation, and synthesis of ideas in reading and writing. It includes locating and critically evaluating sources, as well as using strategies for interpretation, critique, and synthesis to compose texts that integrate the writer's ideas with ideas from sources. Composing processes include strategies for reading, drafting, evaluating, collaborating, and editing. Students should be able to use strategies flexibly for a range of reading and writing purposes. Finally, knowledge of conventions is defined to include not only correct grammar and mechanics but also knowledge of genre conventions for organization and language.

The CWPA, together with the National Council of Teachers of English (NCTE) and the National Writing Project (NWP), included these outcomes in a Framework for Success in Postsecondary Writing (2011). In addition to these knowledge and skill outcomes, the framework includes habits of mind such as curiosity, creativity, persistence, responsibility, and metacognition.

Metacognition is defined to include reflection on one's own thinking, on the processes used in writing, and on applying their learning in future projects. Such metacognitive reflection is needed to handle the complexity of writing tasks and take control of one's learning (Harris & Graham, 2009; Zimmerman & Risemberg, 1997).

SUPPORTING STRATEGIC WRITERS PROJECT

The Supporting Strategic Writers (SSW) project was formed with the goal of improving writing instruction and outcomes for postsecondary students. Thus, since 2010, our research group (MacArthur et al., 2015, 2022, 2023; MacArthur & Philippakos, 2013, 2021) has been working collaboratively with community college faculty to develop instructional approaches for developmental writing and integrated reading/writing courses and then to test them in rigorous experimental studies. Our research over 10 years has consistently found strong effects on students' writing quality and on their motivation.

The goals of the SSW approach are aligned with the outcome goals of the CWPA (2011). We understand that students need knowledge of academic writing genres; strategies for critical reading, planning and revising; and the habits of mind that support continued critical reading and writing in the future. Therefore, the instructional approach addresses not only the teaching of strategies for writing and reading but also the development of metacognitive skills and knowledge that can equip students to reflect and transfer knowledge across contexts of learning. The program targets not only the development of writing skills but also the development of independent writers who can apply the strategies across courses and be successful and confident.

The SSW instructional approach is based on strategy instruction with self-regulation (Harris & Graham, 2009; MacArthur, 2011). The fundamental concept behind strategy instruction in writing is that students can learn cognitive and metacognitive strategies based on the processes used by proficient writers. Research in elementary and secondary schools has shown that strategy instruction has a strong positive impact on writing quality (Graham et al., 2016). Many of these studies have focused on teaching planning strategies based on text structures or genres (Englert et al., 1991; MacArthur, 2011; MacArthur et al., 2015). The most extensively studied approach, the self-regulated strategy development model (Graham et al., 2016; Harris & Graham, 2009), employs metacognitive strategies such as goal setting and progress monitoring, which have been found to enhance learning outcomes (Graham et al., 2016). Effective teaching methods include providing explicit explanations, using think-aloud modeling to make cognitive processes visible, and offering collaborative or guided support to promote independence.

A few studies have investigated strategy instruction for writing with college students, though not in developmental courses. Nussbaum and Schraw (2007) used a graphic organizer to guide integration of arguments and counterarguments and taught evaluation criteria for an argument that emphasized integration. Zhang (2013) taught text structures for informative and problem–solution essays and how to use them for both reading and writing. Two studies by a research group in Spain (Granado-Peinado et al., 2019; Mateos et al., 2018) taught college students a strategy for writing an argument based on sources; the studies used key features of strategy including explanation and think-aloud modeling of strategies and collaborative work. All of these studies reported substantial effects on the quality of writing (for a review, see MacArthur, 2023).

In the SSW approach, students learn strategies based on the rhetorical purposes, text structures, and linguistic features of genres. Genre elements integrate the strategies for planning and revising, as well as critical reading and note-taking. The strategies provide an initial map for students unsure about how to engage in the writing process. Equally important, students learn metacognitive strategies for goal-setting, task management, progress monitoring, and reflection. Journaling and class discussions engage students in reflecting on how they can take control of their own learning through setting goals, selecting strategies, and monitoring progress. Self-evaluation and reflection on one's progress are critical to developing a growth mindset (Yeager & Dweck, 2012) that learning is possible with effort and strategic choices. Pedagogical methods include discussion of model essays, think-aloud modeling of strategies, collaborative writing, peer review and self-evaluation, and reflective journaling. The core concepts and practices of SSW are explained in Chapter 2.

RESEARCH ON SUPPORTING STRATEGIC WRITERS

Our research began with design studies in collaboration with community college faculty. We conducted three semester-long cycles of design, implementation, evaluation, and revision over 2 years (MacArthur & Philippakos, 2013). The design research also included development of a measure of motivation for writing that assessed four aspects of motivation: goals, self-efficacy, beliefs, and affect (MacArthur et al., 2016). We found large gains from pretest to posttest in writing quality. More important, we refined the instruction based on feedback from instructors and students.

Following the design research, we conducted a quasi-experimental study (MacArthur et al., 2015) with two colleges, 13 instructors (16 classes), and 276 students (48% minority, 10% non-native English speakers). Classes using the experimental SSW curriculum were compared to control classes that received typical instruction for a full semester; classes were not randomly assigned but were comparable on demographics and pretest writing. The SSW curriculum had a large effect on quality of argumentative writing, but no significant effect on grammar. It also had a large effect on self-efficacy (confidence) and a moderate effect on mastery motivation.

With a second grant from the U.S. Department of Education, we conducted a more rigorous experimental study (MacArthur et al., 2022) with two community colleges, 19 instructors randomly assigned within college to the SSW treatment (T) and control (C) groups, and 207 students (57% minority, 12% nonnative English speakers). Once again, the SSW approach had a very large effect on quality of writing (the average treatment student performed at the 90th percentile of the control group). It also had a positive effect on a standardized writing assessment. As before, we also found a positive effect on self-efficacy for writing.

To this point, the research had focused on writing without sources. However, for college success, students need to write using sources. Therefore, we did a semester of design research (see Philippakos et al., 2021 on design-based research) to extend the instructional approach to include strategies for critical reading and note-taking, writing summary-response papers, and integrating source information into argumentative essays. The design research was conducted with partner colleges that had already participated in the studies of writing without sources.

This design research was followed by a rigorous experimental study of the SSW curriculum focused on writing using sources (MacArthur et al., 2023). The research design was similar with two colleges, 23 instructors, and 187 students participating for a full semester. The study found positive effects on quality of argumentative writing with sources, as well as quality and inclusion of main ideas on a summary. However, no effects were found on motivation, which we think was due to the greater difficulty of writing with sources.

To address current policy efforts to accelerate completion of developmental writing, one of our doctoral students (Nefferdorf, 2020) conducted a quasi-experimental study of an adapted version of the course that met 4 days a week for 4 weeks at the start of the semester, leaving time for an 11-week FYC class. Five instructors (2 T, 3 C) and 65 students participated. The SSW approach had a large effect on the quality of argumentative essays with sources.

Note that in all of these studies, all instruction was provided by college faculty who received an instructors' guide, student books, and professional development (PD). Instructors received 3 days of PD prior to the semester, in which the strategies were explained and modeled and the instructors practiced modeling them and received feedback. During the semester, instructors were observed and coached, and project staff were available to answer questions.

CONCLUSION

> Students who previously had perceived that circumstances controlled them, now saw themselves as the actors in their own successes.
>
> —interview with a participating instructor

This statement shared by one of our collaborating instructors demonstrates the "breaking of the writing curse" that students who attend developmental writing classes often face. Students who believe that they cannot write well often deal with their anxiety by doing the minimum needed to get a passing grade. They may even respond to anxiety in self-defeating ways by not submitting assignments or dropping the course. Through instruction designed to support early successes and develop self-evaluation and self-regulation strategies that help them see their successes and manage the writing process, they are able to be writers and own their own success confidently.

In closing, we would like to make three points. First, our research provides strong evidence that Supporting Strategic Writers has substantial positive effects on the quality of writing in developmental writing or integrated reading/writing courses. Dozens of studies have found positive effects of writing strategy instruction in elementary and secondary schools, and our research extends the results to college.

Second, we worked collaboratively with college faculty for many years to design and redesign instruction that fits the college context and meets the needs of instructors and students. Subsequent to our research studies, we have continued to collaborate with our partner colleges and instructors to make improvements to the curriculum and help them better adapt it to their colleges. Most of the collaborating instructors who used the SSW approach continued to use it after completion of the studies. Two of the colleges that participated in the research studies adopted SSW as their approach for developmental writing courses, and we helped them provide PD to new instructors.

Third, although the research has focused on developmental courses, we believe that many of the practices would work well in other courses that require writing. Several instructors have used the strategies and emphasis on metacognitive self-regulation in other courses, including FYC and other humanities courses. Adaptations for other courses will be discussed in Chapter 8.

CHAPTER 2

Core Instructional Components of Supporting Strategic Writers

> Once you have your tasks and your plan or strategy set, you will be more likely to stay focused on completing your tasks and follow your plan. This is because it's your strategy, and you know what tasks need to be done, and how to do them.
>
> —reflection from a student journal

This quote illustrates the improved confidence and sense of mastery that comes from developing a strategic approach to writing. The student has learned some writing strategies for planning; furthermore, they perceive the strategy as their own strategy that helps them get work done effectively. The quote captures the integration of writing strategies that guide writing processes like planning with metacognitive strategies for managing tasks to achieve goals. Unlike so many new postsecondary students, this student feels in control of their writing process.

The goals of our work on the Supporting Strategic Writers (SSW) project are common to college composition courses—that students will develop rhetorical knowledge of audience, purpose, and genres; strategies for critical reading, planning, and revising; and the motivational beliefs that support continued critical reading and writing in the future (Council of Writing Program Administrators, 2014). In the SSW program, students learn systematic strategies for planning, revising, and critical reading based on genres. Further, they learn metacognitive self-regulation strategies for goal setting, task management, progress monitoring, and reflection. In this chapter, we explain the core principles of the SSW instruction and introduce the writing strategies, metacognitive strategies, and pedagogical methods used in the program.

CORE PRINCIPLES OF STRATEGY INSTRUCTION

The central idea behind strategy instruction is that the cognitive and metacognitive strategies used by proficient writers, readers, or learners in any challenging domain can be taught in some form to less proficient learners (MacArthur, 2011; Pressley & Harris, 2006). Writing is a complex social and cognitive process that requires content knowledge, knowledge of the social and rhetorical situation, knowledge of genres commonly used in various situations, and strategies for using that knowledge to set goals, generate and organize ideas, make appropriate linguistic choices, and evaluate and revise the work. In addition, because of its challenging nature, writing makes substantial metacognitive and motivational demands. Writers need to set goals, choose strategies, manage time and task, maintain their motivation, and evaluate progress. Writers develop metacognitive strategies to meet these demands and maintain their productivity.

For example, suppose I decide to write a letter to the editor in response to a recent article about declines in academic achievement during the COVID-19 pandemic. I am not surprised by the declines, but the recent data gives me an opportunity to make some recommendations about what the government might do to manage the problem. I head off to my home office to think and write. In setting goals, I consider purpose, audience, and the genre of "letters to the editor"; I also think about how to present myself and my expertise. I know that a letter to the editor needs to reference something that appeared in the paper, be brief and get to the point quickly, and be written in an accessible and engaging style. With all this in mind, I generate ideas and begin drafting. For such a short form, little attention is needed for organization other than to start by referring to the article. When I get stuck, I resist the impulse to get another cup of coffee by reminding myself that it's a short piece that I can finish if I stick to it. I look back at the draft repeatedly to see how it reads, and when the draft is done, I go through it again, asking myself questions about clarity, appeal to likely readers, and strength of the message. Overall, I bring together my personal motivation, knowledge of the genre of "letters to the editor," rhetorical goals, strategies for content generation and evaluation/revision, and metacognitive strategies for task management and progress monitoring.

The knowledge about writing and the cognitive and metacognitive strategies used in this brief example can be taught to less experienced writers. In fact, a large body of research with students in elementary and secondary schools has shown that it is, indeed, possible to substantially improve the quality of writing by teaching cognitive and metacognitive strategies (Graham et al., 2012; Graham et al., 2016; MacArthur et al., 2015; Traga Philippakos, 2019; Traga Philippakos & MacArthur, 2021; Traga

Philippakos et al., 2019). Our own research, summarized in Chapter 1, has extended those findings to college.

A well-designed program of strategy instruction can provide an integrated way to help students develop the rhetorical knowledge, writing strategies, and metacognitive strategies needed for successful independent writing. Strategy instruction draws on multiple theoretical and empirical sources to address three design issues: *what strategies to teach, how to support independent writing and learning*, and *what pedagogical methods are needed* (MacArthur, 2011; Philippakos et al., 2015; Philippakos & MacArthur, 2020). First, the design of the *writing strategies* themselves uses research on the cognitive processes of proficient writers and research about common academic genres. Second, research on *metacognition and motivation* supports methods for developing independence. Finally, research on strategy instruction provides guidance about *pedagogical methods* for helping students develop the strategies. We address each of these in the following sections.

WRITING STRATEGIES

The design of writing strategies draws on research on the cognitive processes of proficient writers (Hayes, 1996; MacArthur & Graham, 2016) and on research about written genres and their purposes, organization, and linguistic features (Rose, 2016). Strategies are goal-directed cognitive processes for challenging tasks. Strategies range from general strategies to domain-specific strategies. General strategies, like brainstorming, apply broadly across many problems and situations, but they have limited power. Brainstorming can be made more specific and powerful by combining it with discourse knowledge about genres, for example, generating ideas for an argumentative essay by brainstorming ideas that might be held by people on both sides of an issue. Thus, domain-specific writing strategies usually are based on a combination of knowledge about genres and knowledge about writing processes.

Proficient writers have rhetorical knowledge about the purposes of writing for various audiences and the genres appropriate for those purposes and contexts (MacArthur & Graham, 2016; Philippakos, 2018). They use that knowledge strategically for planning, drafting, evaluating, and revising. When planning, they engage in rhetorical analysis to set goals and use their genre knowledge to help generate and organize ideas (Hayes & Flower, 1980). When revising, they apply evaluation criteria relevant to their goals and the type of writing (MacArthur, 2016; Philippakos & MacArthur, 2016). Most research on instruction in writing strategies teaches students to plan or revise using knowledge about particular types of text, or genres (Englert et al., 1991; Graham et al., 2012). For example, early research on strategies used story grammar structure to teach both reading (Dimino et al., 1990) and writing (Graham & Harris, 1989). To our knowledge, the first research on writing strategies based on expository genres was by Englert and colleagues (1991). They also used text structure to integrate planning and revising strategies. Their planning strategy involved analysis of the writing task, brainstorming, and selection of a graphic organizer with an appropriate text structure (e.g., comparison, persuasion) to organize their ideas. For evaluation and revision, students learned to use evaluation rubrics specific to the genres.

SSW Writing Strategies

The SSW approach teaches students to use genre-based strategies for critical reading and writing. The strategies use knowledge about the rhetorical purposes, text structures, and linguistic features of genres (e.g., argument, causal explanation) to guide planning and revising, as well as critical reading and note-taking. The full set of strategies is designed to support writing an essay with sources (see Figure 2.1). The strategies include the familiar processes of planning, drafting, and revising; they also include strategies for critical reading and note-taking, and integration of ideas when writing using sources. Subsets of the strategies can be used to write essays without sources or summary-response papers on single sources.

In this section, we explain the strategies in the case of argumentative writing with sources. An argument is intended to persuade others to support a position on a controversial issue. The organizational elements include the issue, position, reasons and evidence, counterarguments with rebuttals, and conclusion (see Figure 2.2).

The first strategy, "Begin with your own ideas," includes rhetorical analysis of the writing task and brainstorming to generate ideas from prior knowledge. Students use the mnemonic TAAPO to analyze a writing task for Topic, Audience, Author, Purpose, and Organization. The TAAPO analysis emphasizes consideration of audiences that might disagree about the issue. The brainstorming uses a T-chart for generating reasons on both sides of an issue, prompted by questions about people with differing opinions and rebuttals for ideas generated (see Figure 2.3). The brainstorming chart also includes space for questions that students can pursue in reading sources.

The second strategy, "Understanding what others say/Critical reading," guides the process of critical reading and note-taking. It requires two readings. The first reading focuses on rhetorical analysis of the source using the TAAPO mnemonic. An important part of TAAPO is considering the credibility of the author and source. The source articles used are generally argumentative, either arguments for a position or discussions of arguments on

Core Instructional Components of Supporting Strategic Writers

Figure 2.1. Writing Strategies

Supporting Strategic Writers
WRITING STRATEGIES

Begin with your own ideas
- Analyze writing task with TAAPO
- Brainstorm with Idea T-Chart

Understand what others say/Critical reading
- Analyze source with TAAPO
- Close reading
- Take notes on the Argument GO

Integrate ideas from sources with your own
- Discuss ideas
- Display your notes
- Use Idea T-Chart
- Decide what you want to say

Plan your essay
- Organize ideas with Argument GO
- Keep track of sources to cite them

Draft
- Use your plan
- Write clear topic sentences for main ideas
- Provide supporting details

Revise and edit
- Evaluate and revise
- Edit for errors

both sides. The second "close reading" is guided by the argument elements. Students read a paragraph at a time, looking for argument elements; they highlight and annotate key elements and use an Argument graphic organizer (GO) to take notes (see Figure 2.4). Students are taught that in published articles, the argument elements may be in any order; for example, an op ed piece might start with rebuttal of opposing reasons and end with the author's position. Thus, they may need to search for the elements to comprehend the article. Note that the GO includes a space for evaluative comments

Figure 2.2. Elements of Argumentative Writing (IROC)

I	**Introduction**	
	Issue: What is the issue? Why is it important?	
	Position/Thesis: What is your position?	
R	**Reasons and Evidence**	
	Clear reasons: Give reasons for your position	
	Supporting evidence: Support your reasons with facts, examples, and explanations.	
O	**Opposing Position**	
	Opposing reason(s): What does the other side have to say?	
	Evidence for opposing reason: Give facts, examples, or explanations.	
	Rebuttal: Say why you disagree. Give your reasons.	
C	**Conclusion**	
	Restate position: Tell what your position is again.	
	Finish with a strong point: Leave the reader with something to think about.	

on the reasons and evidence presented by the author; students use this space to begin their critical analysis of ideas.

The third strategy, "Integrate ideas from sources with your own," addresses the challenges of integrating ideas from multiple sources and one's own ideas to create a coherent argument. Students need to look for connections across the ideas and decide on their position and what reasons and evidence to use. They lay out their notes from the various sources and their own brainstorm and ask questions about points of agreement and disagreement. They use the Idea T-chart, the same chart used for brainstorming, to support this process.

Then in the fourth strategy, "Plan your essay," they select and organize ideas on a new blank Argument GO. As they do this, they keep track of source ideas on the GO, so they can cite them when they write. The fifth step, "Draft," involves following the plan on the GO and elaborating on the ideas. Because students have a clear plan, they can focus on clarity of expression and adding details. Students are supported in drafting by "sentence frames" for common elements. For example, a frame for introducing an opposing position might be "Some people argue (believe, say, think, suggest) that _____."

The final strategy, "Revise and edit," focuses on learning to self-evaluate one's writing, which is critical to improvement in writing. Revision is guided by a genre-specific rubric with questions relevant to arguments, such as whether the issue and position are clearly presented, whether each reason is connected to the position and supported with adequate evidence, and whether opposing positions are presented and rebutted effectively (see Figure 2.5). Peer review is used to help develop students' self-evaluation skill. Finally, students edit for errors and clarity.

Core Instructional Components of Supporting Strategic Writers

Figure 2.3. TAAPO and Brainstorming Chart

TAAPO
- T (Topic)
- A (Author)
- A (Audience)
- P (Purpose)
- O (Organization)

Idea T-Chart

Use for brainstorming and integrating ideas from sources.

Topic or Issue:	
One Side	Opposing Side
What questions do I have?	

When writing without sources, the first strategy, "Begin with your own ideas," is used along with the strategies for planning, drafting, and revising; application of these strategies for writing without sources is discussed in Chapters 3 and 4. One step on the way to writing using multiple sources is to write summary-response papers about single sources. For this, the first three strategies are used (see Chapter 5). Application of the full set of strategies is discussed in Chapter 6.

Figure 2.4. Argument Graphic Organizer (GO)

Use for Note-taking and for Planning Your Own Essay

Citation:			
Issue/Problem:			
Author's position (or central idea)			
Reasons (or main points)	Key evidence (or supporting details)		Comments
Opposing position (if present)			
Opposing Reasons	Support/evidence	Rebuttal	Comments

The strategies in the Supporting Strategic Writers approach for planning, drafting, and revising, as well as the strategy for critical reading of sources and note-taking, all integrate knowledge of the purposes, organization, and other features of academic genres. The big idea behind the strategies is that if students understand the purposes and elements of a genre, they can use that information to guide planning, revising, and critical reading. While the overall strategies remain the same, the details adapt to varied genres; in particular, the graphic organizers and rubrics are based on the elements of the genre. In this way, the strategies are

Core Instructional Components of Supporting Strategic Writers

Figure 2.5. Essay Evaluation Rubric

Writer's Name: _____ Reviewer's Name: _____ Date: _____					
Rubric Score: 0 = missing, 1 = needs work, 2 = strong					
INTRODUCTION	Score				
Issue: Does the *writer* say why the issue is important?					
Position: Is the *writer's* position clear?					
REASONS and Evidence (2 or more)	R1	R2	R3	R4	
Clear REASONS: Is each reason stated clearly and connected to the position?					
Supporting EVIDENCE: Is each reason supported with information from sources or personal experience?					
SOURCE Integration: Are sources integrated with each other and the writer's experience?					
OPPOSING POSITION					
Opposing reason(s): Did writer state the opposing position and provide one or more reasons?					
Supporting EVIDENCE: Are opposing reasons supported with *information* from sources or experience?					
SOURCE Integration: Are sources used to rebut or support an integrated position?					
CONCLUSION					
Restate position: Is *the* position stated in new words?					
Strong point: Does it leave the reader something to think about?					
SOURCE CITATION					
Is information from sources credited and cited?					
Is source *information* written in the writer's own words?					
Other					
Are transition words used effectively?					
Were all assignment requirements met?					
PEER FEEDBACK:					
What was done well?	Suggestions for improvement:				
Writer's Goals: What will I change?					

specific enough to guide writing in a particular genre, but at the same time generalizable across genres. Instructors can teach any genre by analyzing the purpose, organizational elements, and evaluation criteria, and then creating an appropriate graphic organizer and rubric and selecting appropriate sample papers.

METACOGNITION AND MOTIVATION

The second critical aspect of strategy instruction is development of metacognition and motivation. Theories of metacognition, self-regulation, and motivation inform decisions about how to help learners take independent control of their learning and use strategies flexibly (Flavell, 1979; Pajares et al., 2007; Schunk & Zimmerman, 2007; Zimmerman & Risemberg, 1997). The theoretical construct of metacognition (Flavell, 1979) includes knowledge about one's cognitive processes and self-regulation of cognitive efforts. One important aspect of metacognitive knowledge is understanding when, where, and why to use particular strategies and how those strategies can be flexibly adapted to new situations (Pressley & Harris, 2006). In addition, proficient writers understand the challenges of writing and the importance of metacognitive strategies for managing the writing process and maintaining attention and motivation over time. For example, skilled writers manage time and environment (e.g., setting aside three hours in the morning in a home office like I am doing right now), select strategies from their repertoire (e.g., write freely for a time to generate ideas, outline), set productivity goals to stay on task (e.g., finish this section before taking a break), maintain motivation (e.g., think about the goal), monitor progress, and reflect on what they have learned. Less proficient writers often interpret their struggles with writing as evidence that they are just not good writers, but the reality is that all writers struggle with the complexity of writing and need metacognitive strategies to maintain productivity, monitor progress, remain motivated, and learn from experience. These strategies can be learned just like the writing strategies themselves.

Research on writing strategy instruction has shown that integrating metacognitive, self-regulation strategies with cognitive strategies substantially increases the effects on quality of writing (Santangelo et al., 2016; Schunk & Zimmerman, 2007). Explicit attention to metacognitive, self-regulation strategies is a defining component of the self-regulated strategy development model (SRSD, Harris & Graham, 2009). The SRSD model includes instruction in metacognitive strategies for goal setting, progress monitoring, positive self-talk, self-evaluation, and management of time and environment. Extensive research on writing instruction following the SRSD model in elementary and secondary schools has demonstrated substantial effects on writing quality (Graham & Perin, 2007; Graham et al., 2012).

In the college context, metacognitive strategies are often taught as strategies for academic success in separate courses on study skills. We argue that it is more effective to teach such strategies in the context of writing courses that are especially challenging for students. In that way, students can immediately apply the metacognitive strategies and see the power of using them to take control of their own learning. The SSW approach includes a set of metacognitive strategies, the *Strategies for Academic Success*, that includes goal-setting, task management, progress monitoring, and reflection (see Figure 2.6). The strategies can be deployed across each writing task beginning with setting learning goals and ending with reflection on learning and setting of new goals.

The metacognitive strategies play an important role in supporting student motivation. The SSW approach is designed to develop students' metacognitive awareness and to enhance their confidence and motivation. The systematic writing strategies and pedagogical methods provide initial support for students who are uncertain about how to approach writing tasks. The emphasis on metacognitive strategies and self-evaluation helps students

Figure 2.6. Strategies for Academic Success

Supporting Strategic Writers
STRATEGIES FOR ACADEMIC SUCCESS

GOAL SETTING	TASK MANAGEMENT	PROGRESS MONITORING	REFLECTION
What are my long-term goals?	How can I manage my work to get it done?	Am I using the strategies?	How did I do on the task?
What specific goals do I have for this assignment?	What strategies can I use?	Are they helping me to get the job done?	How did the goals and strategies work?
	How can I motivate myself to do my best?	Shall I consider other strategies?	What strategies will I try next time?
			What goals will I set next time?

to see for themselves that their writing is improving in specific ways (Blake et al., 2016;Traga Philippakos & MacArthur, in press). As their confidence increases, they are more willing to engage with challenging writing tasks in order to learn more (Traga Philippakos, 2020a).

One way that we help students to see their progress is to have them compare the baseline essay that they wrote on the first day of class with essays that they wrote using the strategies. Students use the rubric to evaluate the baseline and write a reflection on their progress; they are often amazed at how much they have improved.

One of the students in our research captured the importance of the metacognitive strategies well:

Throughout the semester, I have constantly used goal setting and task management. Planning ahead with a goal in mind helps me to better prepare and succeed. Each task I make sure I plan out what I want to have accomplished each day of the week until the item is due. Constantly planning ahead, I succeed or exceed my intended goal.

—reflection from a student journal

The pedagogical methods that support growth in writing achievement, motivation, and independence are discussed in the next section.

PEDAGOGICAL METHODS

Most composition instructors teach the writing process and some strategies and want their students to become more strategic, but this instructional goal is challenging. The pedagogical methods used in the SSW approach are supported by substantial research on strategy instruction (MacArthur, 2011; Traga Philippakos & MacArthur, 2019), especially research on the self-regulated strategy development model (SRSD, Graham et al., 2016 Harris & Graham, 2009). The general principles of strategy instruction include development of background knowledge, explanation and think-aloud modeling of the strategy, scaffolded practice including collaborative work, and gradual release of responsibility to the students as they gain mastery. In the remainder of this chapter, we explain the key principles of think-aloud modeling and collaborative and guided practice in some detail with examples. We then outline the instructional sequence in SSW for teaching genre-based strategies and metacognitive strategies that can be thought of as a *"strategy for teaching strategies"* (MacArthur & Philippakos, 2013 Philippakos et al., 2015). Chapters 3 and 4 provide examples of how the strategies for planning and revising are applied to genres.

One central challenge for instruction is that cognitive strategies are invisible mental processes. Certainly, it is helpful to discuss models of good papers, to explain strategies, and to give feedback (Graham & Perin, 2007; Hillocks, 1984), but it is not sufficient. In a wonderful story by P. G. Wodehouse (1922), a famous Scottish golf pro goes to the office of a wealthy chief executive and explains how to swing a golf club, whereupon the executive plays in a championship the next day, nearly winning both the match and the girl. The absurdity is obvious, yet we do much the same in writing classes when we explain strategies without demonstrating them.

Most of what we learn in life is through observation of others (Bandura, 1986; Vygotsky, 1978). One of the instructors who worked with us in a research study gave the following analogy in a conference presentation: Whether we want to know how to cook a new French sauce or re-tile the bathroom, we know where to look—videos on YouTube.

The key pedagogical methods of strategy instruction—think-aloud modeling and collaborative writing—are designed to make the cognitive processes visible so that students can learn by observation and reflection. Think-aloud methods were used in early research on writing processes to understand the cognitive and metacognitive processes used by experts (Hayes & Flower, 1980), and they have become a critical element in teaching those processes. In think-aloud modeling, instructors use strategies to accomplish a writing task while verbalizing their thoughts, all live in front of students (Traga Philippakos, 2021). Then instructors lead discussions of what students observed. Students have the chance to learn by observing and reflecting without simultaneously attending to their own writing. After such modeling, instructors and students can engage in collaborative writing, in which the instructor guides students through the strategies and scribes while students generate and organize ideas, draft sentences, and evaluate the work with whatever support they need. This collaborative work provides another opportunity to make the strategies visible with active engagement from students. In the SSW approach, all the strategies—planning, evaluation/revision, critical reading and note-taking, and summarizing source texts—are modeled and practiced collaboratively.

Think-aloud modeling is intended to be a live demonstration of how to apply a strategy to a meaningful task. Instructors explain the strategies before modeling, but students do not really understand them until they observe the modeling. Here are a few key features of effective modeling:

- Think-aloud modeling is more than an explanation with examples. Instructors should prepare in advance by trying out the planning

strategies for the topic they plan to use, but the modeling should be done "live" without notes or prepared examples.
- Modeling should be at the level of a good student. Select a topic about which students will have some information and use language at their level so they can follow your thinking.
- Refer to the strategies throughout the process. For example, ask yourself what the next step is and then apply it. When students try the strategy on their own, they will be following the strategy.
- Modeling should include metacognitive strategies. Talk to yourself about the challenges you face and congratulate yourself when you solve a problem. It is good to "struggle" a bit; it lets students see that even good writers get stuck at times. If you model smoothly without difficulties, students may not see the strategies as applicable to them. Modeling that includes coping with difficulties is more effective than modeling with complete mastery.
- The students may offer suggestions as you ask yourself questions, and you may even solicit suggestions to keep them engaged. But it is important for the instructor to stay in charge of the process. The goal is to give them a model of how to use the strategy well to solve problems.

Chapters 3, 4, 5, and 6 include some examples of think-aloud modeling. The next section outlines the instructional sequence in SSW for teaching genre-based strategies and metacognitive strategies (also in Philippakos et al., 2015; Philippakos & MacArthur, 2020; Traga Philippakos & MacArthur, 2022). We think of this sequence as a "strategy for teaching strategies."

INSTRUCTIONAL SEQUENCE: A STRATEGY FOR TEACHING STRATEGIES

Introduction to the Genre

Instruction is organized into units focused on genres, for example, memoir, procedural, causal explanation, comparison, and argument. Instruction begins with a discussion of the purpose of the genre. For example, the class would discuss when people might use comparison and contrast in writing; it is often used to make decisions or to learn about similarities and distinctions among concepts. The structural elements of the genre are explained briefly.

Analysis of Strong and Weak Examples

Strong and weak samples of the genre are discussed and analyzed. The samples are student essays, not published writing; thus, they represent the expectations of the course. Students discuss the strong example and what makes it strong; they are guided to look for the elements of the genre. For example, for compare-contrast writing, they would look for the categories of comparison. At this point, the evaluation rubric for the genre is introduced by the instructor, and it is used to analyze the strong example. Next, a weaker example is discussed and analyzed for strengths and weaknesses using the rubric. In this way, the evaluation criteria are introduced at the beginning of instruction, contributing to the important goal of developing self-evaluation.

Explanation and Modeling of the Strategies

The instructor explains and models the writing strategy as it applies to the genre. The explanation is fairly brief since students will understand it better when it is modeled. The instructor then applies the strategy using think-aloud modeling. In modeling, the instructor refers to the strategy consistently and models at the level of a good student. It is important to include statements about effort and the metacognitive strategies in the think-aloud. Also, it is important to include planning, drafting, and revising. It is generally possible to model the full planning process and parts of the drafting, returning later to model some evaluation and revision. Students can offer suggestions during the modeling as long as the instructor maintains control to provide a good example of the strategy. After the modeling, the instructor leads a discussion of what the students observed and their thoughts and questions.

Collaborative Practice

After modeling, the instructor and students engage in collaborative writing. The instructor guides the students in application of the strategy and supports them as they analyze audience and purpose, generate ideas, organize, and suggest sentences for drafting. Collaborative writing gives students an opportunity to apply the strategy with a high level of support. It is particularly useful for supporting students in the drafting process as they learn how to construct sentences appropriate to the genre. Collaborative practice can also be used to guide content discussions; for example, debates can be conducted to learn about how to deal with opposing positions in argumentative writing.

Guided Practice

After discussing the purpose and organization of writing in a new genre, analyzing good and weak examples, observing the instructor, and writing collaboratively, students finally write their own papers. Students still need guidance and feedback. In general, it is important to provide feedback and help on the use of the strategy as well as on the written product itself. One direct way to support use of the strategy is to ensure that students memorize the strategies and the genre elements; though memorization is a low-level task, students will not be able to use the strategies if they do not remember them well and easily recall the components.

Peer Review and Editing

When first drafts are completed, students engage in peer review and editing. Peer review provides more collaborative opportunities to make self-evaluation processes visible. Students often resist peer review on the grounds that their peers are not competent to give them feedback (MacArthur, 2016). However, research (Cho & MacArthur, 2011; Philippakos & MacArthur, 2016) has shown that students learn from giving feedback, perhaps more than from receiving it. The process of giving feedback requires application of evaluation criteria to identify problem areas and make suggestions for improvement. This process is exactly what is needed for self-evaluation.

Research shows that peer review is more effective when students are prepared adequately. In the SSW approach, preparation includes think-aloud modeling and collaborative review using papers by unknown peers. Students then work in pairs to evaluate each other's papers, providing scores on the rubric and suggestions for improvement. Since the rubric is focused on the elements of the genre, the feedback can be specific and, thus, easier for the writer to understand and use. Instructors also provide feedback using the criteria on the rubric, sometimes with additional criteria. Instructors have reported that having a rubric that the students understand makes it easier to provide feedback.

Editing is done separately from revision. After students revise for content, the instructor provides needs-based editing instruction, and students may work in pairs to make edits. The instructor conferences with students about errors.

CONCLUSION

Rose (1989) wrote that underprepared writers are well aware of their problems with writing, but they are not sure about how to improve. Their anxieties can create motivational problems that interfere with progress. SSW is designed to give them the strategies they need to tackle critical reading and writing tasks and the metacognitive support needed to begin to take control of the learning process. The strategies are taught explicitly using think-aloud modeling and collaborative practice so that students can observe how the strategies work. The strategies support student success in writing, which provides essential motivation. The metacognitive strategies help students to take control of the writing process by setting goals and reflecting on their progress and on the strategies.

In this chapter, we explained the core principles of strategy instruction with metacognition and outlined the pedagogical methods used in the SSW approach. We provided a rationale for the use of strategies based on genre knowledge and the cognitive processes of proficient writers. We also emphasized the critical importance of developing metacognitive awareness and self-regulation. Finally, we briefly described the Strategy for Teaching Strategies that guided our curriculum design and professional development. The chapters in the next section provide more detailed explanations of writing in multiple genres without sources.

Part II

SSW WRITING STRATEGIES

…

CHAPTER 3

Planning and Drafting for Argumentative Writing Without Sources

"A goal without a plan is just a wish," says Antoine de Saint-Exupéry in *The Little Prince*. This quote could be shared with learners of all ages, and we might use it ourselves to accept a reality: Dreaming does not lead to success without careful planning. Indeed, in the process of writing, planning is critical; the lack of a plan can lead to frustration and to a paper that does not satisfy the needs of the audience and meet the writing purpose. Effective writers carefully analyze a writing assignment or task to devise a plan that meets their goals (Bereiter & Scardamalia, 1987; Hayes & Flower, 1980). In contrast, inexperienced writers tend to immediately begin drafting with minimal time spent on planning.

In Chapter 2, we explained the overall Writing Strategy for writing using sources (see Figure 2.1). In this chapter, we focus on writing without sources, explaining the strategies for planning and drafting and how to teach them following the Strategy for Teaching Strategies. Writing a clear, organized essay without sources is an appropriate goal for many students and a step toward writing with sources. In this chapter, we provide examples illustrating the strategies when working on argumentation. We should note that the strategies can be used when working on many different types of writing. To make the explanation of instruction clearer to readers, we focus on argumentative writing while briefly commenting on ways that the strategies can be used when working on another type of writing such as compare and contrast. Chapter 4 continues with the strategies for evaluation and revision without sources. The overall Writing Strategy described in Chapter 2 includes six strategy components, but the second and third components, about critical reading and integration of sources, are not used when writing without sources. This chapter focuses on three strategy components:

- Begin with your own ideas
- Plan your essay
- Draft

Teachers who work on writing without the use of sources will have the following goals and objectives for their students:

Students will be able to:
- perform a task analysis to identify the assignment's requirements.
- explain the process of task analysis, brainstorming ideas, organizing ideas, and drafting an argumentative essay.

EXPLANATION AND MODELING OF THE STRATEGY

The first two components of the strategy ("begin with your own ideas" and "plan your essay") address what is commonly known as planning. "Begin with your own ideas" includes analysis of the writing task using TAAPO and brainstorming ideas using the T-chart (see Chapter 2 for a thorough explanation). Effective writers carefully analyze the writing task and consider the writing purpose, the audience, the specific question the assignment poses, the genre, and other requirements. Without this analysis, students may misunderstand the assignment and may provide information that is not relevant to the task (Philippakos, 2018). Thus, this analysis is crucial in supporting writers' goal setting. In "Plan your essay," students use a graphic organizer (GO) with the elements of the appropriate genre to select and organize their ideas for writing.

Analyze Writing Tasks Using TAAPO

In SSW we strive to develop learners who can set personal goals for a writing task and produce clear papers that convey their own ideas on a topic. Therefore, students learn how to analyze writing tasks to determine the goals of the assignment. Thus, they examine the Topic, Audience, Purpose, and Organizational elements. They are not examining Author as they are the author of the paper. The acronym TAAPO guides the students in this task analysis. The Audience helps them determine the reader of the task, and Purpose helps them identify the writing purpose and type of writing that would be appropriate for the task. Organizational elements refer to the elements specific to the type of writing or genre on which they are working.

When teaching the writing strategy, instructors will model for students how to begin with their own ideas, plan, and draft their essay. The topic may address a controversial issue that would be interesting to students and would allow the development of ideas on both sides of the argument. For instance, the teacher may present the following writing prompt to students and model by thinking out loud how to analyze it and how to identify their next goals as writers.

Planning and Drafting for Argumentative Writing Without Sources   33

Writing Prompt 3.1

> *Due to a recent increase in vandalism in area parks and playgrounds, many members of the community are demanding the installation of surveillance cameras in these public areas. Others in the community are worried that cameras would limit privacy. Write a paper saying whether you think that surveillance cameras should be installed. Make sure you include clear reasons and evidence to support your position (facts, examples, and explanations).*

To better identify the type of writing the student will complete and in order to develop a clear goal, the teacher will apply TAAPO (see Figure 2.3) and will complete it by examining the information presented in the assignment. When modeling the analysis of the assignment, teachers will read the assignment aloud, and then use the mnemonic TAAPO to carry out the analysis and location of information relevant to TAAPO in the assignment. A sample think-aloud follows:

- **Introduction:** *"I will be modeling for you how write using our strategies. For this purpose, I will be thinking out loud. This means that I will verbalize my thinking so you can hear how I use the strategies, and most importantly how I manage my time and behaviors so I make progress and do not give up. In essence I will model the thinking I would like you as students to do when you work on writing, not only in this class but also in other classes that involve writing. While I think aloud, I would like you to pay attention to what I do and how I do it."*
- **Modeling TAAPO:** *"So, I was given the following assignment, and it is really crucial for me to do well in this assignment. I sometimes tend to rush, so this time, I will use the writing strategy* (see Figure 2.1). *The first task I need to do is begin with my own ideas and analyze the assignment using TAAPO; this will help me understand the assignment and know exactly what I need to do."* [The teacher writes TAAPO vertically on the board or displays the TAAPO form on the screen.]
  - » Topic. *"Okay! Let me read the assignment."* [The teacher reads the assignment out loud.] *"I now need to complete TAAPO, and I will first complete T that stands for topic. What is the topic? Is it about vandalism? Did I understand this correctly? No, I am not sure this is accurate. I need to make sure. Let me reread."* [Teacher rereads.] *"Oh, I see, it is about the installation of surveillance cameras to prevent vandalism. I will write this under Topic so I clearly know what the topic is."* [Teacher writes.]
  - » Audience. *"Who is the Audience for this? Does the assignment explicitly state this? Yes, it refers to members of the community. I will write this as my audience. My audience is also my classmates*

and my teachers who will eventually read the paper and grade it. I will include them, too." [Teacher writes the information.]
» Author. "I will skip this as I am not reading the work of someone else."
» Purpose. "What is the purpose of this assignment? I shall examine the specific question that I am asked to complete. The assignment reads, 'whether you think that surveillance cameras should be installed. Make sure you include clear reasons and evidence to support your position.' I think the purpose is to argue about this issue and whether I think that surveillance cameras are good to have in a neighborhood or not. I should share my opinion with the reader.

The completed TAAPO can be found in Table 3.1.

As teachers think aloud, they not only model how to complete TAAPO and analyze the assignment. Teachers also model how to manage the writing task and how to confirm that they used the strategy appropriately without skipping any of its parts. Thus, monitoring their progress will be something they will embed in their instruction and language as they present the task and its completion.

- **Modeling progress monitoring.** "*Okay, what did I complete so far? I completed my TAAPO and have a good understanding about what the assignment asks me to complete. I now need to proceed with the brainstorm to develop my ideas about the specific topic and whether I think we should or should not have surveillance cameras.*"

Table 3.1. Completed TAPFOR for Writing Prompt on Installation of Surveillance Cameras

T Topic	Should surveillance cameras be installed in public areas of the community?
A Author	The writer
A Audience	Community members, public, classmates, instructor
P Purpose	Persuade/argue
O Organizational Elements	Introduction
Reasons and Evidence
Opposing position
Conclusion

Planning and Drafting for Argumentative Writing Without Sources

The process of analyzing the writing assignment is necessary before diving into the writing task or even before the development of ideas about a writing task. It is easy to be confused when reading writing assignments and especially when writers may be challenged with reading fluency or comprehension. The analysis gives them the opportunity to carefully determine the writing topic so they can develop ideas that are relevant to its question or questions. Identification of the audience for a paper is significant for writing clearly. Knowledge about the audience can determine the tone of the paper and the vocabulary used. Further, it is necessary for writers to determine the purpose of the writing so they can decide how to proceed with the development of ideas. It should be noted that this process of task analysis can be applied across different writing topics that address different writing purposes. Such writing topics may refer to sharing personal experiences, explaining causes and effects, or making comparisons. The analysis of purpose determines the genre, which affects the strategies for idea development, organization, and drafting. In the following example, we present a writing assignment in a genre that is not argumentative to better demonstrate the use of TAAPO.

Writing Prompt 3.2

The change from high school to college. Even if it's your first semester, you have probably noticed that high school and college are different. You can probably remember a bit about your high school experience and what you expected (or didn't expect) from college. For this writing task, imagine you have been asked to compare and contrast high school to college for high school students who are planning to attend college. Your goal is to relate the college environment to their high school world in a manner that they will be able to understand and appreciate.

The task analysis for this topic can be read in Table 3.2.

In this example, there were more *unknowns* that could be crucial for writers' understanding, time, and effort. Through the reading, careful re-reading, and analysis process, writers will reach the conclusion that the audience is prospective college students, the purpose is preparing them for college, and the genre of writing is *compare* and *contrast*.

With goals established by the task analysis, writers can proceed to brainstorm similarities and differences between high school and college and organize their ideas using a graphic organizer for compare-contrast. By reflecting on their own experiences as both high schoolers and first-year college students, they can consider ways that the two contexts are the same or different and provide a response that will address the needs of the readers. Without this careful analysis, writers might have misunderstood the goal of the paper or the type of writing they needed to do.

Table 3.2. Completed TAPFOR for Writing Prompt Comparing High School and College

T Topic	Changes from high school to college
A Author	The writer
A Audience	New college students, high school seniors, classmates, instructor
P Purpose	Prepare high school students for college life and academic expectations
O Organizational Elements	Elements of compare-contrast

Brainstorm With Idea T-Chart

Once learners have identified the writing purpose, they work to generate ideas. Brainstorming allows learners to draw ideas from their background knowledge and their long-term memory. This process does not need to be filtered; rather, it allows learners to generate ideas freely without any judgment. In the process of brainstorming, learners consider what the audience might think so they can better address the thoughts, concerns, and considerations their readers may have about the topic. The goal is not to eliminate any ideas but to generate as many as possible. Even ideas that may not connect well with the topic are valuable because they may lead to clearer and more relevant ones.

Brainstorming connects with the type of writing or genre that is taught. Therefore, in the process of developing ideas, brainstorming will address the core goals of the genre. For example, when writing an argument, brainstorming will involve the identification of alternative positions held by different groups and the development of ideas in favor and against those positions (see Table 3.3 for an example). In the modeling, the instructor will explain why a T-chart is good for brainstorming ideas on both sides and then develop ideas by thinking out loud about the two sides (Philippakos et al., 2015; MacArthur et al., 2015). The development of ideas will be live (i.e., without notes) and will include the instructor developing and recording ideas in front of students. Drawing from the previous example on *surveillance cameras*, we have provided a sample think-aloud on brainstorming.

- **Explaining the use of brainstorming.** *"Since this is an argumentative paper, I will develop ideas for both sides and*

Planning and Drafting for Argumentative Writing Without Sources

Table 3.3. Brainstorming for Topic on Installation of Surveillance Cameras

For: Installation of surveillance cameras	Against: Installation of surveillance cameras
Cameras deter criminal behavior—no vandalism	Violation of privacy
Cameras are used widely around the country	Cost: too much money to purchase-install-use
Allow for accurate identification of perps	Need police presence, not cameras
Increase community safety	Who is monitoring?

examine pros and cons. It is important I consider both sides even though I may be convinced that one of the sides is the one I plan to support. By carefully thinking ideas on both sides, I can develop more convincing ideas for this specific audience. [Instructor draws the T-chart with For and Against or displays it on the board.] *For this topic, I'm not sure yet whether I am for or against the installation of surveillance cameras. Brainstorming what I know and what I think others will say will help me decide on my position."*

- **Brainstorming.** *"Let me think about reasons that people might have on both sides. Well, when people know they are recorded, they may not commit a crime. So, thieves will not want to have cameras installed or people who engage in acts of vandalism in the community. But the residents of the community who pay fees to keep the community in pristine condition would prefer to have those cameras so they can identify the violators. Drawing from the assignment's content, I can say that the presence of the cameras will function as a warning to those who may consider breaking the law. Right? It is rather silly to do something violent when you know you are watched! I will write this idea.* [Teacher writes on the organizer, "Cameras deter criminal behavior—no vandalism."] *But why would some people be against cameras? Well, they might be concerned about privacy."* [Teacher continues brainstorming.]

The teacher in this example develops ideas by first thinking about the topic and the audience, verbalizing thoughts, and recording phrases and some ideas. There is no need to provide complete sentences when recording the ideas as the purpose of brainstorming is to generate as much as possible for the writer to then select appropriate ideas to organize and then write.

At the end of the brainstorming, the instructor will read the ideas on both sides and determine which is the position that is more convincing to adopt. Then the other side with opposing reasons will be the opposing position that the instructor will need to prove is wrong and effectively rebut. After the completion of brainstorming, the instructor will again reflect to examine what was completed and what the next step would be. For this, they may refer to the writing strategy and its components and address the parts that are completed as well as the ones that still need to be completed.

When writing a compare-contrast paper, the brainstorm will involve generating ideas about similarities and differences of the things to be compared (see Figure 3.1 for an example). If students were writing a personal narrative, the brainstorm would include ideas about characters and the setting as well as responses to questions such as "what happened first," "and then what else," "by whom," and "why." When writing a paper about causes (e.g., "what are the causes of procrastination?"), writers will consider why something happens and the explanations of those causes.

Once ideas are developed in the brainstorm, learners review them and then organize and filter the information for it to be placed in a graphic organizer that represents the organizational structure of the genre. Not all

Figure 3.1. Brainstorming for Compare-Contrast

High school		College
-own bedroom, home	-academic skills like reading and writing and math, maybe harder in college	-dorm rooms
-classes all day		-academic expectations higher
-short assignments for homework		-more writing
-friends I've known for years	-parties	-classes 15 hrs/wk
-parents there to help	-grades	-responsible for getting to class
-sports		-on own to get work done
		-sports, intramural
		-all kids are smart

Planning and Drafting for Argumentative Writing Without Sources   39

ideas will be transferred to the graphic organizer to be used at drafting. Each writer will choose their position and select the strongest reasons to support it. At the same time, the graphic organizer prompts writers to select opposing reasons that they can counter with rebuttals. When completing the graphic organizer, learners may cross out the ideas from the brainstorm so they can better keep track of the ideas used and of those combined. This process can help them monitor idea use and avoid repetitions that can affect writing quality. For the example on surveillance cameras, the graphic organizer is in Table 3.4. Teachers will think aloud while completing the graphic

Table 3.4. Completed Graphic Organizer for Topic on Installation of Surveillance Cameras

Issue: Crime in public space and installation of cameras as a way to prevent it					
Position [I say]: To install surveillance cameras		Opposing Position [What others say]: Not to install surveillance cameras			
Reasons [Why I say what I say]	Evidence	Reasons [Why they say what they say]	Evidence	Rebuttal [Why they are wrong]	
Prevent crime	People are less likely to commit crime if they know there are cameras	Privacy	Police and others can see where we go and who we are with	It does cause me to give up privacy, but you don't have a right to privacy in a public setting—safety is more important	
Increased safety	Use of cameras promotes a feeling of a safer community where crime is not tolerated. Cameras are a tool to help police	Cost		Cost of crime: loss of property, life, cost to people in work, policework, to society, versus cost of cameras	
Effective at identifying vandal	I see on the news all the time how people on video get ID'd	Need police presence, not cameras			

organizer and cross out the ideas used from the brainstorm. Therefore, the two need to be close to each other so it is easier to refer to both.

Table 3.5 presents the graphic organizer on compare-contrast.

Depending on the genre, learners will need to consider the audience and its needs. For instance, when working on argumentation, it is important that reasons for the opposing position are rebutted. If this is not done, then

Table 3.5. Compare-Contrast Graphic Organizer

Introduction	*Tell why the topic is important.*
	Purpose/Thesis Statement:
Body Paragraphs	Point/Category 1:
	Provide details
	Point/Category 2:
	Provide details
	Point/Category 3:
	Provide details
Conclusion	Restate Purpose/Thesis:
	Strong Ending:

Source: Zoi A. Philippakos & Charles A. MacArthur, 2015, *Developing Strategic Writers Through Genre Instruction. Resources for Grades 3 to 5*. Adapted with the permission of Guilford Press.

Planning and Drafting for Argumentative Writing Without Sources

the writer's argument will not be convincing. Consequently, students will need to not only identify a reason for the opposing position but a response to that reason. Students may select to consider a reason they have already developed as a response to rebut the opposing position, or they may think of a new idea. The greatest need is for students to consider a response to the opposing position that strengthens their argument and identifies flaws to the reasoning of the opposing side.

Draft

At the drafting stage, writers need to utilize their plan, apply sentence frames (if and when they need to do so), and develop their sentences. Not all students will need to use sentence frames. Their function is for students who may find writing challenging, who may not be familiar with linguistic forms used in the genre, and who may need some help to transform the words from their graphic organizer to sentences for drafting (see Figure 3.2 for sentence frames used for argumentation and Figure 3.3 for sentence frames used in compare-contrast).

When modeling how to develop sentences, instructors should consider using different sentence formats and state them orally so students can observe how phrases and words are translated into sentences (see Philippakos, 2022). At this stage of the writing strategy, the ideas are represented in sentences and paragraphs. A sample think-aloud modeling is included in this section; however, depending on the needs of the students, different emphasis on sentence construction may be given.

- **Draft.** *"So, now I need to write my paper. This process should be really easy since I have all ideas on my organizer; I will also use sentence frames to develop my sentences. I also need to make sure that I indent. It is easier to develop the Position and will begin with this. I can return to the introduction and write it when I also write the message to the reader at the end. Okay! I can use different sentence frames for the position, but I think I will say, In my view, surveillance cameras are necessary for the public good and should be installed.* [Teacher types.] *I will now move to a new paragraph and intent as I will need to develop my first reason. Let me look in my graphic organizer. As a first idea, I have the prevention of vandalism. I will begin the topic sentence by saying, One reason. No, actually, I will emphasize and say, 'One important reason to install surveillance cameras is that they would control vandalism.' This is a good sentence, but I wonder if I could make it a bit more specific. What if I say, get vandalism under control and make sure it doesn't escalate. This sounds clearer."* [Teacher types.]

Figure 3.2. *Sentence Frames for Argumentation*

For Positions
- I think that _____.
- In my view, _____.
- From my perspective, _____.
- My response to this issue is _____.

For Reasons
- One reason I think _____ is _____.
- Another reason I think _____ is _____.
- An additional reason is _____.
- In addition, _____.
- Also, _____.
- Next, _____.
- Furthermore, _____.
- Moreover, _____.
- Finally, _____.

Three Steps to Writing an Effective Opposing Position Paragraph

Step 1: What does other side have to say?
- Some people argue (believe, say, think, suggest) that _____.
- On the other hand, some readers think (believe, say, suggest, claim) that _____.
- _____ (a group or person) believes that _____.
- However, some people disagree with _____ (your position). They claim (say, suggest, think) that _____.

Step 2: Provide supporting evidence for why they think that way with facts, examples, or explanations.
- One example they give is that _____.
- They support their position by saying that _____.

Step 3: Then give your rebuttal. Say why you disagree. Give your reasons.
- However, _____ (evidence against their reason).
- Even though _____, I argue that _____.
- Although _____, I still maintain that _____.

For Conclusion
- In conclusion, _____.

Using the information from the previous example on surveillance cameras, the modeled paper may take the following form (see the accompanying box text on the following page):

Planning and Drafting for Argumentative Writing Without Sources 43

Figure 3.3. *Sentence Frames for Compare-Contrast*

- For introduction of points:
  One way that . . .
  One point to consider is . . .
  A second way that . . .
  Another point to consider is . . .

- For addition of details:
  In addition,
  Also,
  Further,
  Furthermore,
  Moreover,

Source: Zoi A. Philippakos & Charles A. MacArthur, 2015, *Developing Strategic Writers Through Genre Instruction. Resources for Grades 3 to 5*. Adapted with the permission of Guilford Press.

SAMPLE COMPLETED ESSAY FOR TOPIC ON SURVEILLANCE CAMERAS

Recent acts of vandalism in our neighborhood community parks and playgrounds have raised concern about crime in our community. People are worried that if left unchecked, this will lead to crime getting worse in these areas. In recent years, many cities have begun using surveillance cameras in public areas to prevent crime. Many members of our community have suggested the installation of cameras as a response to the recent acts of vandalism in our parks and playgrounds. While installing cameras raises concerns for some community members, **in my view**, surveillance cameras are necessary for the public good and should be installed.

One important reason to install surveillance cameras is that they would get vandalism under control and make sure it doesn't escalate. The vandalism hasn't been a one-time incident, and it is getting worse, resulting in destruction of property. If cameras are installed, people are less likely to commit a crime, knowing that someone is monitoring the area via video surveillance. Cameras can be a powerful deterrent and will allow the police to stop the problem before it becomes more widespread. With installation of cameras, both the community and law-breakers will see that surveillance provides results.

Furthermore, installation of cameras promotes a safe environment. Some community members are concerned that the vandalism may make people stop coming to the public spaces, and it could escalate to crimes against people. The use of cameras will send a message that our community does not tolerate crime. While police officers do community policing in these areas, it is not enough. They come by in cars, on bikes, and by foot regularly and talk with the residents, but they cannot be there all the time. Cameras would be an additional tool for the police to use to promote safety in our community.

Another reason that surveillance cameras should be installed is that they are effective in identifying the perpetrators of vandalism. Across the country, from major cities to small towns, communities are installing cameras as a tool to help police officers. The cameras don't replace the police but can provide assistance by being on duty 24/7. Cameras can provide actual video of a criminal act when no witnesses are present or can support or discredit a witness accounting. Video can be used to identify perpetrators when their identities are not known. The police often release video and ask for the community's help to anonymously identify suspects. Often viewers recognize the suspects and come forward, which can substantially shorten police work.

Others may argue against installing surveillance cameras and raise concerns about invasion of privacy. They would say the police would have access to the video, and others might get access without proper permission. Opponents of surveillance argue that citizens have a right to go where they please in the community and walk and talk with anyone without others knowing about it. **While it is** true having cameras in public areas does mean we may be videoed, in this age, we have to balance an expectation of a right to privacy in a public setting with the need for public safety.

In addition, some might say cameras mean a significant cost for the community. They claim the purchase, installation, and monitoring of cameras will be a big expense for taxpayers. Some think paying for the presence of a police officer for a couple of nights would be a better deterrent to vandalism and other crimes than a camera. However, the continuing high cost of crime, including loss of property, cost to people in lost wages, extra policework, and court costs far outweighs the cost of purchasing and installing cameras.

In conclusion, the installation of surveillance cameras in our community is necessary. Protection of public property is a priority and, in our community, where many people don't have yards, the parks and playgrounds are widely used public spaces. Recreation centers hold basketball leagues and youth programs in the parks, children play on the playgrounds, and community members walk and run there. The use of surveillance cameras in our community public areas hit by vandalism is a cost-effective investment that serves as a deterrent to crime. Installing cameras will promote a feeling of a safe community where crime is not tolerated, and you can't put a price on that.

An important caveat about modeling: During modeling, instructors should develop a paper that represents the level that students are expected to achieve; thus, they should avoid using vocabulary that may be unknown to students and can also be disengaging to them. Also, it is important for attention to be on the strategy used, on the sentence frames, and on the formation of meaningful ideas in sentences, not on grammar alone. If there is a shift to overcorrection of grammar when students brainstorm, the emphasis is not on the planning and drafting but rather on editing.

Closure of Modeling

After teacher modeling, students and teacher engage in a conversation about what was observed. Specifically, the teacher will ask students to share whether what they observed the teacher do was familiar to them, whether it was helpful, and what components were familiar or helpful. Then teacher and students will discuss the specific strategies used and the key purposes of those strategies. For example, for the completion of the task analysis, it was important to determine the audience as a way to decide on the language and tone used for the essay. When working on brainstorming, it was necessary to entertain all ideas and include all ideas. When drafting, it was important to use the sentence frames. Teacher and students review the writing strategy and the components they would use when working on a writing topic.

COLLABORATIVE PRACTICE

After modeling, the instructor and students engage in collaborative writing to plan and write an essay on a new topic. For this collaborative work students will work with the teacher, whose role is to support students as they navigate the use of the strategies and to scribe the information. The specific objectives teachers will have for students are the following:

- Students with teacher support will perform a task analysis to identify the assignment's requirements.
- Students with teacher support and guidance will explain the key organizational elements of argumentative writing: a clear position, reasons with support, consideration and rebuttal of opposing positions, and a conclusion.
- Students with teacher support and guidance will brainstorm ideas using the T-chart, organize them, and draft an argumentative essay.
- Students with teacher support will monitor their writing progress and application of strategies.
- Students will reflect on their work and effort and consciously determine the ways strategies support them as writers.

The collaborative lesson will begin with a review of the purposes of argumentative writing and of the elements of argumentative writing. The class will also review the writing strategy and discuss the importance of completing the task analysis, brainstorming, and organizing before drafting an essay.

Then the teacher and students will proceed with collaborative planning and drafting. Throughout the process, the teacher will ask questions about the strategies and engage students in responding.

The teacher will present a topic or engage students in a discussion about a topic and ask them to share what would be the first task they need to do before they begin writing. The first strategy would be to begin with your own ideas, which includes analysis using TAAPO and brainstorming. The teacher will record TAAPO and ask students to share what the topic, author, audience, purpose, and organizational elements would be for the specific topic. Next, the class works together on the Planning step using the GO. Finally, they work together or in groups to draft the essay. As students respond, the teacher clarifies, questions, scaffolds, and records the information. Thus, the task is done collaboratively, but if students need additional support the teacher will offer it, and if needed, the teacher may provide some modeling.

At the end of the collaborative task, teachers and students discuss the use of the strategies and how they support students as writers. The teacher may ask students to respond to the following questions as a way to reflect on the writing strategies' use and on students' anticipated challenges with the writing strategies and writing overall.

- How could the writing strategies support me as a writer and help me achieve my writing goals?
- What are the ways that TAAPO can help me as writer?
- Why would it be helpful for me to brainstorm and organize my ideas before I write?
- What are the challenges I have as a writer, and how can these writing strategies support me?

Students may discuss their responses as a group or with a partner. Further, as they progress within a semester, they may be asked to return to reread these responses and examine how their use of the strategies has changed or their writing has progressed.

GUIDED PRACTICE

After teacher modeling and collaborative practice, students proceed to work on their own on a new writing prompt. For this task, they may be asked to complete the TAAPO and brainstorm for more than one topic.

Then they may be asked to work on the topic they have sufficient information about and can elaborate on comprehensibly. The main challenges students will face, besides the use of these strategies, is that they will need to rely on their background knowledge. Thus, it is important to examine the writing prompts and select those that they can write about with the knowledge they have. The specific goals and objectives targeted at guided practice are as follows:

- Students will perform a task analysis to identify the assignment's requirements.
- Students will brainstorm ideas using the T-chart, organize them, and draft an argumentative essay.
- Students will monitor their writing progress and application of strategies.
- Students will independently write well-developed argumentative essays that are clearly organized and in which errors do not interfere with fluent reading and understanding.
- Students will reflect on their work and effort and consciously determine the ways strategies support them as writers.

CONCLUSION

The strategies in the SSW approach help students to plan and draft essays in multiple genres. The strategies begin with TAAPO to help students analyze the writing task and their own goals. Then they use brainstorming to generate ideas freely and a graphic organizer specific to the genre to organize their ideas prior to drafting. Thus, when they work on argument, they consider both perspectives and sides of an argument. Drafting involves the translation of ideas from the graphic organizer to sentences that clearly communicate meaning to readers. During drafting, sentence frames and transition words that respond to genre needs can support students who need them. In reference to strategies, one of the instructors who took part in our experimental study shared,

> I thought that the strategies were so neat. They were tidy and compact and easy to remember. I kept telling the students, "you've got this tool that you can put in your pocket and use from now until the end of your academic career." I think the compactness of the strategies and the, I don't want to say simplicity, but it was . . . they were easy to remember, they were very obvious and straightforward, and I think it was an easy way for students to connect to the writing process. [Also,] it was very easy for me to point to those strategies and for the students to say, Oh yeah, you know what, I was really rushing and I didn't do my IROC, or I didn't do a few of the elements. And I think it made them feel like they understood and they had some clear ownership of the writing process.

> I think that is probably the biggest positive of the curriculum. For them to know that they're part of it. And they can know and grab onto it and run with it. It was really, really useful.

This instructor response indicates how the clarity in the presentation of the strategies supports not only instructors' delivery but also students' ownership. Through the modeling and collaborative practice, students have the opportunity to observe and participate with guidance before they begin their own paper. The guidance of the task analysis and the connection between the elements of the genre, the idea development, the graphic organizer, and sentence development promote students' independence and instructors' teaching efficacy.

CHAPTER 4

Evaluating and Revising for Argumentative Writing Without Sources

At the heart of writing is revising. That is because revision entails careful evaluation of the ideas the author has recorded and their connection to the writing purpose and to the audience. In the Supporting Strategic Writers (SSW) program, we place a strong emphasis on evaluation and revision. The process of working on revisions can lead the writer to discover additional ways to express their ideas and as a result significantly improve their paper (MacArthur, 2016). Further, we believe that writers learn as much, if not more, from giving feedback and evaluating the work of other learners using specific criteria that guide their attention to evaluation as they learn from receiving feedback.

In this chapter, we explain the strategies and instructional procedures for evaluation and revision, the final component of the Writing Strategies (see Figure 2.1). We first explain the strategy for evaluation and revision. Then we explain how evaluation is taught in preparation for peer review and applied to self-evaluation. For instruction in evaluation and revision, the goals and objectives would be the following:

- Students will explain the purposes of evaluation to revise argumentative essays.
- Students will evaluate the work of peers during peer review and offer suggestions for revisions of their argumentative essay.
- Students will self-evaluate their work and identify areas for improvement.
- Students will make at least one revision.
- Students will set goals for improvement on the next paper.

STRATEGIES FOR EVALUATION AND REVISION

In SSW, we devote substantial effort to teaching students how to evaluate their own work and how to peer review. Review is based on the use of specific evaluation criteria that refer to a type of writing, or genre (Philippakos,

2017; Philippakos & MacArthur, 2016). Drawing from the work of Englert and colleagues (1991), we apply the elements of a genre to planning, drafting, and evaluation. Thus, when writers reread their work, they examine the presentation and clarity of specific elements of the genre. In the case of argumentation, the emphasis and attention will be on the IROC elements (see Figure 2.2). Therefore, the reviewer will examine whether the paper has an issue stated, a position, reasons and connected evidence, an opposing position with reasons and a rebuttal, and a conclusion that restates the position and ends with a strong point. In addition, the reviewer will examine other aspects of writing that can affect clarity (see Figure 2.5). Such aspects address the use of transition words and the completion of requirements set by the assignment topic (e.g., length).

The evaluation is conducted using a rubric that has the elements of argumentation and a rating scale to offer a numerical value to each of the elements under examination. Thus, a score of 0 means that the element is missing; a score of 1 means that the element needs improvement, and a score of 2 means that the element is strong. If a reviewer has recorded a score of 0 in the position statement, this would mean that their peer would need to provide a thesis statement that states their opinion on the issue under examination. The use of the numerical system can easily communicate the intentions for revision as the numbers address the clarity of the elements as they are communicated to readers.

INTRODUCTION TO A NEW GENRE

The evaluation criteria and rubric are introduced to students as part of the initial lessons on a new genre. As explained in Chapter 2, instruction in a new genre begins with a discussion of the purposes of the genre and examples of the genre that would be familiar to students. For example, for argumentative writing, the purpose would be explained as persuasion, and the class might discuss political advertisements and opinion pieces in newspapers. Next, the instructor displays a good example of a student essay, discusses what makes it good, and then introduces the rubric for the genre and uses it to evaluate the good paper. The process is repeated with a weak student example.

PREPARATION FOR PEER REVIEW

For students to be able to use the evaluation criteria and to effectively engage in peer review, they need some explanation of the purposes and procedures. Otherwise, they will avoid being critical and honest about the work of their colleagues. This lack of honesty can result in distrust among partners and gradually invalidate the process and value of peer reviewing as a critical aspect of writing. Therefore, significant attention is given to preparing students for peer review and revision. The procedures for peer review preparation are explained here.

- **Explanation of reasons for peer review.** The teacher discusses with students the reasons for peer review and its benefits. The teacher explains that writers learn by giving feedback as well as by getting feedback. When they give feedback, they are analyzing and evaluating someone else's paper, which is a great way to learn about good writing. The process of critical reading and evaluation helps them develop their own essay, as they learn from the challenges faced by their partners and are better able to craft their work with clarity. Further, the process of giving feedback to a peer is the same as self-evaluating their own writing.
- **Explanation of the peer-review process.** The teacher explains that in peer reviewing they will follow a specific process that will allow each writer to share their work with their reader/reviewer before they each proceed with the evaluation of the other's paper. The process used is the following:
    » Both partners read their papers aloud.
    » Each reviewer re-reads their partner's paper silently, identifies the elements, evaluates using the rubric, and writes suggestions.
    » Partners meet and discuss suggestions.
- **Explanation of the rubric and modeling of evaluation and revision.** The teacher discusses the evaluation rubric and explains how it reflects the organizational elements of argumentative writing. Then the teacher models the evaluation procedure using a paper written by an unknown student writer. Modeling of the process includes the following:
    » Teacher displays the Evaluation Rubric for Argumentative Writing (IROC) (see Figure 2.5). Since this is work without the use of sources, the section of the rubric that addresses sources will be ignored.
    » The teacher displays and reads the sample student paper aloud. Students should have a copy to follow along (see the sample paper in the accompanying text box on the next page).
    » The teacher underlines the key elements: position and reasons (see Figure 4.1), discusses the clarity and adequacy of the information, and refers to the evaluation rubric and assigns a numeric score for each element (see Figure 4.2).
    » The teacher examines all scores for elements, identifies the weaker elements, and makes written suggestions for improvement (see end of Figure 4.2).

> **SAMPLE PAPER FOR EVALUATION DURING PREPARATION FOR PEER REVIEW**
>
> Talking and Driving
>
> Technology is rapidly changing and making our lives at times easier and at other times more complicated. Cell phones are one type of technology that is rapidly improving our connections to one another. When a person has a cell phone, it is possible to connect with one another immediately, making communication faster than ever before. However, it is not always a good idea to answer your cell phone immediately. One of the biggest issues with cell phone use is trying to combine it with other activities, namely driving. Using your cell phone while driving is dangerous.
>
> The first reason why using a cell phone while driving is dangerous is because this makes it difficult to coordinate your motor skills. It is not possible to text and watch the road at the same time. A person has to switch their eyes from watching the road and the cars around them to pushing little buttons on a screen or phone. Trying to coordinate these skills is difficult and means that the person is effectively only doing one thing successfully at a time. This results in a delayed response to something on the road, which could have violent consequences.
>
> The second reason why talking and driving is dangerous is that it distracts you mentally. Imagine that while you drive you hear your phone ringing. You search your passenger seat for your phone and then answer the call. Your best friend has broken up with his girlfriend. You try to help him out, when you realize too late that the car in front of you has slammed on its brakes. Mentally, you were not there to react to the hazards on the road.
>
> Some drivers argue that texting and driving is a matter of choice. Therefore, the driver has the right to decide to use or not to use their phone, and no one should restrict that right. But careless users of phones may cause an accident. Driving and talking on a cell phone is something that is seen more and more frequently on the roads of our cities.

» The teacher comments on the specific revisions that the unknown writer of that paper would need to make and then chooses one suggestion to make an actual revision. For instance, in the example provided (see Figure 4.2), the teacher may revise the element of *restatement of the position*. Thus, the teacher may record "In conclusion, talking on a phone while driving is dangerous and should be prohibited by law." Teacher and students may work to identify other possible ways to restate the position.

Figure 4.1. Sample Paper in Preparation for Review With Elements Identified

Talking and Driving

Technology is rapidly changing and making our lives at times easier and at other times more complicated. Cell phones are one type of technology that is rapidly improving our connections to one another. When a person has a cell phone, it is possible to connect with one another immediately, making communication faster than ever before. However, it is not always a good idea to answer your cell phone immediately. One of the biggest issues with cell phone use is trying to combine it with other activities, namely driving. **Using your cell phone while driving is dangerous.** — Issue / Position

    The first reason why **using a cell phone while driving is dangerous is because this makes it difficult to coordinate your motor skills.** It is not possible to text and watch the road at the same time. A person has to switch their eyes from watching the road and the cars around them to pushing little buttons on a screen or phone. Trying to coordinate these skills is difficult and means that the person is effectively only doing one thing successfully at a time. This results in a delayed response to something on the road, which could have violent consequences. — R1 / Evidence

    The second reason why talking and driving is dangerous is that it distracts you mentally. Imagine that while you drive you hear your phone ringing. You search your passenger seat for your phone and then answer the call. Your best friend has broken up with his girlfriend. You try to help him out, when you realize too late that the car in front of you has slammed on its brakes. Mentally, you were not there to react to the hazards on the road. — R2 / Evidence

    Some drivers argue that texting and driving is a matter of choice. Therefore, the driver has the right to decide to use or not to use their phone, and no one should restrict that right. But careless users of phones may cause an accident. — Opposing Position & Reason

    Driving and talking on a cell phone is something that is seen more and more frequently on the roads of our cities. — Strong Point ?

» The teacher and students may work together on additional revisions. For example, they may work on the rebuttal, which is a challenging component of argumentative writing.

» At the end of this process, the teacher models how the writer would work to determine their goals for their next paper. Thus, the teacher will discuss the importance of setting personal goals for improvement and why and how this step is essential for academic success. In the example provided, a goal for the writer may be to thoroughly address the opposing position paragraph, making sure that they include the reasons for the opposing position with evidence and a rebuttal.

Figure 4.2. Completed Evaluation Rubric

Evaluation Rubric: Argumentative Essay

Writer's Name: _____ Reviewer's Name: _____ Date: _____				
Rubric Score: 0 = missing, 1 = needs work, 2 = OK, 3 = strong				
INTRODUCTION	Score			
Issue: Does the writer say why the issue is important?	3			
Position: Is the writer's position clear?	1			
REASONS and Evidence (Paragraphs 2–4)	**R1**	**R2**	**R3**	**R4**
Clear REASON: Does each topic sentence give a clear/accurate reason?	3	3	NA	NA
Supporting EVIDENCE: Is each reason supported with facts, examples, or explanations?	3	2	NA	NA
OPPOSING POSITION				
Opposing reason(s): Did the writer state the opposing position and provide reason(s)?	3			
Evidence for opposing reason: Is each opposing reason(s) supported with facts, examples, or explanations?	0			
Rebuttal: Does it argue against specific reasons/evidence?	0			
CONCLUSION				
Restate position: Is the position stated in new words?	0			
Strong point: Does it leave the reader something to think about?	1			
USE OF SOURCES				
Is information from sources credited and cited?	NA			
Were sources evaluated for credibility? (Ask your peer)	NA			
Is source information written in the writer's own words?	NA			
Other				
Are transition words used effectively?	3			
Were all assignment requirements met?	NA			
PEER FEEDBACK:				

What was done well?	Suggestions for improvement:
- The writer used transition words to present the elements. - The reasons and evidence were well developed and clearly presented.	- Include evidence for the opposing position. - Include a rebuttal for the opposing position. - End the paper by restating the position. - Include a strong point.
Writer's goal: What will I change?	

Student Practice of Peer Review

After the completion of teacher modeling, students work collaboratively with their teacher to evaluate another paper and make at least one revision as a group. The teacher may ask students to work with a partner to evaluate a paper of an unknown writer to practice evaluation and how to offer suggestions, or learners may work as a group or even individually to evaluate, make suggestions, and practice making a revision.

In the selection of papers, teachers may select samples from previous years and remove identifiers so papers are indeed unknown. The only caution would be to select papers that reflect the elements of the type of writing that they are working on and that have some weaknesses so learners can practice their evaluation skills and work on revisions.

PEER REVIEW AND REVISION

Immediately after the completion of this practice reviewing, learners meet with a partner to evaluate each other's work. Each student meets with two partners, one at a time, for peer review of their essays they brought to class. Thus, each student gives feedback on two papers and receives feedback from two peers. We suggest that teachers use a printed version of the rubric as the use of printed forms makes the management of the process easier for students. The forms have space for the writer's and reviewer's names.

In addition, we suggest that teachers collect the peer-review forms with students' final papers and drafts so they can see whether students offer suggestions to one another, what challenges they may face with the evaluation process, and what teachers may need to reteach prior to the next peer-review session.

REFLECTION

Once students complete their peer-review meetings, it is important for them to reflect on the task and on their learning. In this process of evaluation and revision, the reflection at the end with goal setting is based on the scores and performance of the writer (Traga Philippakos, 2019; Philippakos & MacArthur, in press). The rubric functions as a tool for formative assessment so learners identify specific areas of need and target those for the next papers. In addition, teachers can track students' progress across papers and inform their own practice and explanations in future meetings.

Teachers and students may engage in a conversation as a group, and students should be given the space to share their surprises, their challenges, and their learning points. Further, students may be asked to respond in journals to share their experience and reflection about the process of evaluation and what they learned from the feedback of their reviewers and from their experience as reviewers and readers of the work of writers. In this reflection process, students may be given questions to reply to in their journals or may be asked to record their thoughts in general terms about the reviewing process. Some possible questions for discussion and for journal entries may be the following:

- What have you learned from practice evaluating argumentative essays and from giving and receiving feedback from your peers? What (if anything) surprised you, and what did you find helpful?
- Compare the peer review comments with your self-evaluation comments. Did you grow in your skill of reading as a reviewer?
- How did the process of reading and evaluating the work of a peer using this rubric support your understanding about how to revise argumentative papers?

CONCLUSION

The Revise strategy has taught me a more efficient way to evaluate my work as others give me constructive criticism to let me know what I could do better. It allows me to self-evaluate myself better along with peer review and hearing it from the instructor as well.

—reflection written by a student participant

The comments shared by this student reflect the power of revision and structured peer-reviewing procedures. Students feel able and competent to engage in constructive discussions with others and also critically read their own work to make changes that can improve the quality of their written work. The process of evaluation sharpens learners' reviewing and reading skills. It is anticipated that learners may have to overcome previous experiences with evaluation and revision that they had encountered during schooling. In our research, for instance, we learned that students did not value the process of peer review because they thought that their peers did not know enough to offer effective feedback; thus, they only valued the feedback offered by the teacher. This information helped us make revisions to our program to better scaffold and structure peer review and preparation for it. The main change we made was to emphasize that learning to evaluate their peers' papers and provide suggestions for revision would help them to self-evaluate and improve their own papers. In addition, many students' past experiences with revision emphasized editing and grammar; consequently, many of them considered reviewing and revision to address changes in sentences, spelling, and grammar. It was important to address this misconception for students to allocate their attention and effort to content-level changes instead of error corrections.

It is important to consider that teacher modeling is essential in this process of preparation and of student reviewing. Because of previous experiences students may have about rereading and giving feedback, it is necessary for them to observe and listen to how the teacher makes sense of the information in the essay and how each element is evaluated. If this process is not followed, it is likely that students will superficially read a paper and assign a score that does not reflect the quality of the elements and will not be helpful to the writer.

CHAPTER 5

Challenges of Writing Using Sources; Summary-Response

Chapters 3 and 4 focused on helping students learn to write based on background knowledge without sources. Such learning can be valuable for students. It allows them time to focus on generating and organizing ideas, drafting text, and learning to self-evaluate their work and revise for content and conventions. In the context of a single college course, focusing on writing without sources also allows time to write several essays across multiple genres and to develop increased confidence in their writing ability.

However, for success in college, students need to read source materials critically and synthesize information across sources to write their own essays (Council of Writing Program Administrators, 2014; Wolfe, 2011). Writing using readings is a common college task (MacArthur, 2023). First-year composition courses generally require essays or research papers based on sources. In disciplinary courses, much writing is assigned with the purpose of increasing students' content knowledge and critical thinking in the discipline, and research shows that writing about reading does enhance content learning. Even writing about single texts can promote attention and deeper processing of content. Systematic reviews of research have shown that writing summaries, or even answering questions about readings, improves content learning (Graham et al., 2020) and reading comprehension (Hebert et al., 2013). Writing using multiple sources has potential to enhance critical thinking by requiring students to evaluate, compare, and synthesize ideas from multiple perspectives.

Writing using sources is cognitively challenging, requiring the integration of reading, writing, and critical thinking (MacArthur, 2023 MacArthur & Traga Philippakos, 2022; Traga Philippakos et al., in press). Writers need to synthesize ideas from multiple sources with their own prior knowledge to meet the purposes of their own writing (Perfetti et al., 1999). An early theoretical framework for synthesis writing (Spivey, 1990) includes three processes: organizing, selecting, and connecting. Synthesis across sources requires organizing information for each source, making connections through comparison and evaluation in light of the rhetorical purposes of authors, and then selecting and organizing ideas for writing. The SSW strategies for critical reading and integration of ideas address these three processes. The *critical reading* and *note-taking* strategy guides students to identify key ideas in a source and organize them using the elements of arguments. Once the ideas are organized in this way, it is easier to make connections across the sources by comparing reasons and evidence using the strategy for Integration. Finally, students use the T-chart and Argument GO to select and organize ideas to include in their own essays. This process is explained in more detail in the following paragraphs.

Richter and Maier (2017) contrasted strategic and nonstrategic approaches to using sources for argumentative writing. In a nonstrategic approach, writers read to find information that supports their prior beliefs and tend to produce one-sided writing. We have observed this approach in many college classes: Students decide on their position and reasons and read sources with the limited goal of finding some evidence or a quote that supports that position. In contrast, a strategic approach requires understanding that the task involves consideration of opposing viewpoints and strategies for integrating perspectives. A strategic approach requires some degree of openness to alternative positions.

The research base on instruction in source-based writing is growing. Two recent reviews (Barzilai et al., 2018; van Ockenburg et al., 2019) each included 15–16 studies in secondary or college settings. Both reviews identified effective instructional activities that are common aspects of strategy instruction, including the use of graphic organizers to organize source information and make connections across sources, modeling of integration processes, and collaborative discussion. For example, Nussbaum and Schraw (2007) used a graphic organizer to guide integration of arguments and counterarguments and to encourage students to consider the possibility of finding an integrated position. Mateos and colleagues (2018) used a graphic organizer with space for arguments and evidence on both sides, and questions about how each side would refute opposing arguments.

SSW STRATEGIES FOR WRITING USING SOURCES

The strategies for source-based writing in SSW are focused on argumentative writing because of its central importance to academic writing and intellectual development. Argumentative writing engages students in understanding and critiquing source texts written from multiple perspectives. Students must learn to find sources, evaluate their credibility and usefulness, comprehend them, take notes, and integrate ideas from varied sources with their own ideas to write an argument with a coherent perspective.

In the SSW approach to writing with sources, students first learn to write summary-response papers about single sources. This activity provides students with repeated practice in comprehension and critical evaluation of source texts. Writing summaries has been shown to improve both comprehension and writing (for reviews, see Graham et al., 2016; Hebert et al., 2013). In addition, summary-response papers requiring critical reflection on readings are a common type of assignment in disciplinary courses. The critical reading and note-taking strategies involved in writing summary-responses lead naturally to the full strategy for writing an essay that requires synthesis of ideas across sources.

The overall goals of instruction in writing with sources also include metacognitive outcomes:

- Students will learn to read sources critically, take notes, and write summary-response papers.
- Students will independently write well-developed argumentative essays with sources that are clearly organized and in which errors do not interfere with fluent reading and understanding.
- Students will develop as independent writers and students who take control of their own learning through setting goals, selecting strategies, managing tasks, monitoring progress, and reflecting on their effort and learning.

In Chapter 2, we provided a brief overview of the full set of strategies for writing using sources. Chapters 5 and 6 together explain the strategies and instructional methods for a course with the learning goal of writing essays with sources. In this chapter, we explain the strategies and instruction for critical reading and writing a summary-response paper. Chapter 6 continues with explanation of the strategies for synthesizing ideas from sources and planning, drafting, and evaluating/revising an essay with sources.

INSTRUCTION FOLLOWING THE STRATEGY FOR TEACHING STRATEGIES

Introduction to Essays With Sources

The instructional sequence follows the Strategy for Teaching Strategies (see Chapter 2). Here we assume that the overall learning goal is to write argumentative essays with sources, and that writing summary-response papers is a means to that end. Instruction begins with a discussion of the purposes of argumentative writing and the elements of an argumentative essay. The purpose of an argument, whether oral or written, is to persuade others to agree with a particular position on a controversial issue by providing reasons, evidence, and explanations. In writing an argument, it is important to consider alternative positions on the issue and how to respond to the reasons that others might offer to support an alternative position. Then the elements of argument (see Figure 2.2) are introduced and discussed. The class then discusses examples of arguments that students are familiar with, such as political debates or local issues at the college. The instructor can also ask about types of argument relevant to students' majors (e.g., legal arguments, or scientific arguments about medical treatments).

Next, the instructor leads a discussion of a model student essay with sources and introduces the evaluation rubric; the class then discusses and evaluates a weaker student essay. A sample good student essay is shown in the accompanying box text. The discussion of the good essay helps students see how an essay is organized using the argument elements, with the issue and position in the first paragraph, reasons and opposing reasons in topic sentences, and a conclusion. It is also an opportunity to discuss how source information is used to support an argument and the importance of citing sources. The discussion also introduces the evaluation rubric, which includes questions about sources (see Figure 2.5). For both the good and weak essay, the instructor guides students in finding the elements and then using the rubric to evaluate them. As part of this discussion, the instructor points out the challenges of using sources, namely that students will need to learn to read sources with a critical eye, take notes, and figure out how to use ideas from sources in their own essays.

SAMPLE GOOD STUDENT ESSAY

Electronic Media and Young Children
By Charles Allison

Americans of all ages are plugged into electronic media like never before. People text and surf the Internet on their smart phones, connect with friends and families on Facebook, check facts on Google, and spend hours watching their favorite TV shows. Perhaps, it is natural then that parents, anxious to give their youngsters every advantage, would look to technology to educate their young children. Many buy electronic media for their infants and turn on educational television for their preschoolers. However, the truth is that TV and other electronic media might interfere with children's learning (Kang, 2013).

One reason that time spent watching TV and using other electronic media is a problem is that it takes time away from activities that are truly important for children's learning. According to the National Research Council (2015), the first two years of life are critical for development of language, social interaction, motor skills, and curiosity about the world. This is when babies and toddlers (0–2) develop language skills by interacting with their parents and others about what is happening around them. Young children learn about the physical world by playing with clay and blocks and by running and climbing in the playground. They develop their imagination by building forts out of blankets with other children and adults. No video or app can possibly interact with youngsters in these rich ways.

Another reason that use of electronic media should be limited for young children is that parents are their children's most important teachers. Research shows clearly that one of the best predictors of success with reading and school is the time that parents spend reading and talking with children about books (O'Keefe, 2014). Love of books comes from cozy lap time with parents. Reading with children can be highly interactive. Parents and children talk about the characters and the story as well as the pictures and words. Children point and ask questions. All this interaction is critical to language development (O'Keefe, 2014).

Some argue that electronic media made for very young children by PBS, Disney, and other name brands are educational and interactive. Many parents see technological change as progress and believe that technological toys must be improvements on old-fashioned blocks and dolls and toy cars. Young children are often content to sit and play with media or watch videos for a long time. On the one hand, parents think if an app, computer game, or educational TV can keep their child happy, then the child must be learning something and getting prepared for the future (Kang, 2013). O'Keefe (2014) argues that a young child's imagination is stimulated more during play with others than through screen time. Also, a child's language develops best by talking with the adults and peers in their immediate world (O'Keefe, 2014).

Young children learn through play and interaction with the people in their lives. No technological toy or app can replace the attention of parents, siblings, and friends. So turn off the TV and computer games and go play with your children. Read with them, play with them with their toys, and have conversations about what is happening.

References

Kang, C. (2013, August 14). Toy industry seeks to defend benefits of apps for children, but scientific evidence is scant. *Washington Post.* https://www.washingtonpost.com/business/technology/toy-industry-seeks-to-defend-benefits-of-apps-for-children-but-scientific-evidence-is

-scant/2013/08/14/f5e77a80-04f7-11e3-88d6-d5795fab4637_story.html?utm_term=.99f466f657f0

National Research Council. (2015). *Transforming the workforce for children birth through age 8: A unifying foundation* (L. Allen & B. B. Kelly, Eds.). Washington D.C.: National Academies Press. https://www.ncbi.nlm.nih.gov/books/NBK310550/

O'Keefe, L. (2014, June 24). Parents who read to their children nurture more than literary skills. American Academy of Pediatrics. https://www.aappublications.org/content/aapnews/early/2014/06/24/aapnews.20140624-2.full.pdf

Note: Charles Allison is a first-year college student; he wrote this essay for a psychology class.

Supporting Strategic Writers Project: MacArthur, C. A., & Traga Philippakos, Z. A., 2021.

Introduction to Summary-Response Papers

Next, the instructor explains that in order to learn how to read critically, take notes, and write about ideas from sources, students will start by writing about single source articles, that is, they will write summary-response (S-R) papers. The S-R paper, as we recommend teaching it, includes a one-paragraph summary of the article followed by a paragraph of critical response. Separating the summary and response encourages or requires students to focus first on what the author said, that is, to listen, before responding critically. The summary begins with an introductory sentence with information about the author and source and the position (or central idea if the source is not an argument). The rest of the paragraph gives the main ideas—reasons and key evidence as well as opposing reasons and rebuttals if present. The response provides the student's evaluation of the strengths and weaknesses of the author's argument and comments on the credibility of the source. The sentence frames provide support for concise presentation. As with all writing tasks in SSW, an evaluation rubric is based on the elements of the summary-response genre.

The instructor presents and evaluates a good example of a student summary-response (see the accompanying box text), along with the elements of a summary-response paper (see Figure 5.1) and the rubric (see Figure 5.2). The good example of summary-response is about one of the sources cited in the good student essay; this is not necessary, but it helps students see the connection between the summary-response and essay. The discussion of the good summary-response paper follows the same general procedures as the good essay.

Challenges of Writing Using Sources; Summary-Response   65

Figure 5.1. Elements of a Summary-Response Paper

SUMMARY

Introductory Sentence
- Author and source: Who is the author? What is the title or source?
- Position (or central idea): What is the author's position?

Main Idea Sentences
- Reasons: Give reasons or other main points.
- Evidence: Include **only** the most important evidence.
- Address opposing reasons and rebuttal (if present).

Remember
- Use your own words to present the author's ideas (not your ideas).
- Be clear that the ideas are the author's.
- Cite the author.

RESPONSE
- Evaluate the strengths and weaknesses of the author's argument.
- Give your response to the author's ideas.
- Comment on the credibility of the author and source.

COMPLETED SUMMARY-RESPONSE ON O'KEEFE (2014)

In an article in *AAP News*, the journal of the American Academy of Pediatrics (AAP), O'Keefe (2014) argued that reading books to preschoolers improves their language skills, early reading skills, and parent-child bonds. The article discusses a new policy from the AAP stating that pediatricians should tell parents about the importance of reading aloud to their children. O'Keefe mentions research showing that reading to young children prepares them to learn to read in school. In addition, the author claims that parent-child interaction while reading helps children develop language and cognitive skills. Pediatricians can influence parents by explaining the importance of reading aloud. The article also notes that some parents may think that very young children are not ready for reading. A pediatrician responds that it is important to read appropriately with very young children by talking about the pictures and asking questions. Encouraging more reading is especially important for low-income parents who are less likely to read to their children.

The article presents a new policy from the major professional organization for pediatricians, so it is highly credible. The author says that the claims are supported by research and uses quotes from experts. The research is not explained at all, and it would be interesting to know more about it. I agree that it is important to read to children from an early age. I can see that some people might think it's a waste of time to read to a 3-year-old, but the author makes a good point about reading appropriately for age. I think talking about books and pictures will keep children interested.

Figure 5.2. Evaluation Rubric for a Summary-Response

Writer's Name: _____ Reviewer's Name: _____ Date: _____ Rubric Scoring: 0 = missing, 1 = needs work, 2 = OK, 3 = strong		
Citation:		
Introductory Sentence	Score:	Comment:
• Are author and title or source given?		
• Is author's position (or central idea) clearly stated?		
Main Idea Sentences		
• Are the reasons (or main points) stated clearly and accurately?		
• Is only the most important evidence offered for support?		
• Are opposing reasons and rebuttals summarized, if present?		
Other Summary Features		
• Is it clear the ideas are the author's?		
• Is it written in the writer's own words?		
• Does it cite the source correctly?		
Response Elements—In the evaluative response, does the writer:		
Evaluate the author's reasons and evidence?		
Respond to the author's ideas?		
Comment on the author and source?		

Source: Zoi A. Philippakos & Charles A. MacArthur, 2015. *Developing Strategic Writers Through Genre Instruction. Resources for Grades 3 to 5.* Adapted with the permission of Guilford Press.

Explanation and Modeling

Next, the instructor provides a brief explanation of the full set of strategies for writing using sources (see Chapter 2). The goal is for students to understand the overall plan of the strategies and why each of the strategies is important. Students will understand the details of how the strategies work when you model them later. It is important to point out that the first two steps will be used in planning for a summary-response. If students have already learned the strategies for writing without sources, this explanation can focus on the steps for critical reading and integration of ideas from sources.

Following this overall explanation, the instructor models the first two strategies, which lead to writing a summary-response.

Begin With What You Know

The first strategy, "Begin with what you know," has already been explained in Chapter 2. What is important at this point is explaining that brainstorming activates prior knowledge for critical reading. Thinking before reading about what they already know and what questions they have prepares them to think critically about what the authors say. It's also important to think about their existing opinions so that they can keep an open mind when reading.

Understand What Others Say/Critical Reading

The strategy for critical reading, "Understand what others say/Critical reading," involves at least two readings. The first reading focuses on rhetorical analysis of the source using the TAAPO mnemonic. Students read to understand the overall topic (T); to consider the credibility of the author and source (A); and to figure out the intended audience (A), purpose (P), and organization (O). The source articles selected are generally argumentative, either arguments for a position or discussions of arguments on both sides. If an article is not an argument, students might still read it to find information they could use in their own argument. The second close reading is guided by the argument elements. Students read a paragraph at a time, looking for argument elements; they highlight and annotate key elements and use the Argument GO to take notes (see Figure 2.4). Note that the GO includes a space for evaluative comments on the reasons and evidence presented by the author; students use this space to begin their critical analysis of ideas. The space can also be used to ask questions about things to check in further reading. It is important in modeling the note-taking process to comment on the importance of using one's own words in taking notes. Students should only copy text if they find a quotation they really want to use, and quotation marks should be used. Using their own words not only avoids potential accidental plagiarism, it also supports their comprehension as they express ideas in terms they understand.

In preparing to model the strategy for students, instructors should apply the strategy themselves, carrying out all the steps including rhetorical analysis and brainstorming on the topic, repeated readings of a source article to analyze TAAPO and then taking notes on the argument GO, and finally writing the summary-response. However, the modeling should be done "live," without referring to notes. Remember that thinking aloud is the heart of strategy instruction; it makes your cognitive processes visible to students. Students learn more from models who get stuck and use the writing strategy and metacognitive strategies to problem solve and overcome the challenges. Discuss the challenges, and also comment on your successes and how the strategies helped you.

We have provided completed examples of an annotated source article, notes on the argument GO (see Figure 5.3), and a summary-response paper. In this example, the writing topic was about whether online education will improve learning. The strategy starts with "Begin with what you know," which includes TAAPO and brainstorming; this part of the strategy was explained earlier. It is important to include it in modeling writing with sources because activating students' prior knowledge on a topic is important before reading.

ANNOTATED NOTES ON SOURCE 1 ON ONLINE LEARNING

The Rise of Online Learning
Ilker Koksal, *Forbes*, May 2, 2020

Online learning has shown significant growth over the last decade, as the internet and education combine to provide people with the opportunity to gain new skills. [Reason] Since the COVID-19 outbreak, online learning has become more centric in people's lives. The pandemic has forced schools, universities, and companies to remote working and this booms the usage of online learning.

About the market

There are numerous online learning platforms in the market such as Udemy, Coursera, Lynda, Skillshare, Udacity that serve millions of people. [Evidence] While Skillshare is mostly for creatives such as giving courses on animation, photography, lifestyle, Coursera is mostly academic with giving access to university courses.

Top tier universities are also democratizing the learning by making courses accessible via online. [Evidence] Stanford University and

Harvard University give access to online courses under categories of computer science, engineering, mathematics, business, art, and personal development.

These all show one thing, there's a huge demand from people to learn online. **The reason for this demand and rapid growth of the market with a wide variety of platform options for different groups of people may be the rapid change of the world. [Reason]** People need new work skills. The president of Udemy, Darren Shimkus says, "The biggest challenge is for learners is to figure out what skills are emerging, what they can do to compete best in the global market. **[Evidence—quote]** We're in a world that's changing so quickly that skills that were valued just three or four years ago are no longer relevant."

Advantages of online learning

All those online learning enterprises have a massive amount of user data which enables those platforms to use machine learning algorithms that can enhance the learning patterns of people. [Reason] For example, when a student repeatedly struggles with a concept at the course, and the platform can adjust the e-learning content to provide more detailed information to help the student.

Another big advantage is also time. **People can arrange their schedules according to their convenience and this enables them to scale themselves. [Reason]** This represents a huge opportunity for entrepreneurs to increase their knowledge assets rapidly. "While the online learning industry is growing at a rapid pace, it is now key to stay up to date with the latest developments. This is an incredible opportunity for those who go the extra mile," Javid Niazi-Hoffmann, coaching consultant from Germany who is convinced of the power of online learning, states.

The cost structure of online learning is another factor for the rapid growth of the market. **Online courses prove a more affordable option than traditional ones [Reason]** and there are no commuting costs, and sometimes required course materials, such as textbooks, are available online at no cost.

It's a fact that online learning is the future and will undoubtedly replace land-based learning in the future. [Position] Mobile platforms have given access to more people to benefit from online learning, and this has created a huge data, then machine learning has given personalized solutions to the course content with using the big data. In the future, it will not be surprising to see more elements in the online learning structure such as VR/AR or more advanced machine learning algorithms to democratize the learning more.

From Forbes. © 2024 Forbes. All rights reserved. Used under license.

Figure 5.3. Completed Example of Notes on Source 1 on Online Education

Analyze the Source Using TAAPO
    T (Topic): online learning
    A (Author): Ilker Koksal/Forbes
    A (Audience): general/business
    P (Purpose): to convince people that online education is the future
    O (Organization): persuasive/main idea at end

Close Reading: Take Notes Using the Argument Graphic Organizer (GO)

Citation:
Koksal, I. (2020). *The rise of online learning.* Forbes. https://www.forbes.com/sites/ilkerkoksal/2020/05/02/the-rise-of-online-learning/?sh=1257f8a472f3

Issue/Problem: Is online education the future of education?
Author's position (or central idea): Yes, online education is the future because of multiple advantages. (At the end of the article)

Reasons (or main points)	Key evidence (or supporting details)	Comments
Online education has grown dramatically over 10 years.	There are lots of different online programs. Important universities offer online classes: Harvard and Stanford.	One of my friends got a degree in computer science and got a job right away.
People want online education to keep their skills current for work.	Online education is the easiest way for most people to get access to lots of classes, according to Darren Shimkus (President, Udemy).	But the quote is from president of a company that sells online platform.
The data that learning platforms collect on students allows the platforms to help people learn.	The example offered is when a student keeps getting an idea wrong, the software adapts to offer more explanation.	I'm not sure about this.
Scheduling is flexible, so people can learn what they need to at their own rate.	Flexibility is important for business people.	Another quote from the business.
Online education is less expensive.	Classes are cheaper. People don't have to pay for gas or parking at school. Sometimes class materials are free online.	This makes sense.

Opposing position (if present)
No opposing position offered.

Opposing Reasons	Support/evidence	Rebuttal	Comments

Challenges of Writing Using Sources; Summary-Response 71

> **SUMMARY-RESPONSE ON SOURCE 1 ON ONLINE LEARNING**
>
> In his article, "The Rise of Online Learning," Ilker Koksal (2020) asserts that the future of education is online learning because of the multiple benefits to people. The first reason that Koksal offers is that online education has grown dramatically and is even used in major universities. Next, Koksal argues that people want education to keep their skills current in a world of changing work. One of the most important reasons that Koksal offered is how technology can be adapted to help students learn more, like faster feedback, software offering more detail for concepts that students don't get, and maybe even virtual or augmented reality in the future. The last reason that Koksal offered was the lower cost of online classes. The classes themselves are often more inexpensive, and there are no costs of driving or parking and often no costs associated with textbooks either. Koksal did not offer any opposing positions.
>
> Koksal's assertion that online education is the future is weakened by the lack of an opposing position. Koksal did not consider any of the many good reasons why people don't think online education is a good idea for everyone. Not everyone has access to their own computer or to fast enough Internet to make online education work for them. Also, his evidence is mostly statements from leaders in the online education business, who are biased. Still, most of the points Koksal made as to why there are advantages in online education are good ones, especially the one about how education will be accessible to more people and more kinds of learners in the future. Everyone having access to educational choices that appeal to them is really important for an educated population.
>
> **REFERENCE**
>
> Koksal, I. (2020). The rise of online learning. *Forbes*. https://www.forbes.com/sites/ilkerkoksal/2020/05/02/the-rise-of-online-learning/?sh=1257f8a472f3

One of the source articles selected by the instructor is an article in *Forbes* (2020) arguing that online education is far better than traditional university classes. The box text, "Annotated Notes on Source 1 on Online Learning" shows the article (shortened for space) with highlighting and labeling of key argument elements, and Figure 5.3 shows the TAAPO and completed notes on the argument GO. In analyzing TAAPO, one should note the credibility of the source; *Forbes* is a well-known publication focused on business. The main audience is business leaders and others with an interest in business.

On the first reading, students should identify the purpose, which in this case includes the position taken by the author, which is stated most clearly *at the end of the article*, namely, that online education is the future and will eventually replace traditional courses.

In the close reading, readers search for the argument elements. They are highlighted and labeled in the text; in live modeling, the instructor might include more annotations. The article starts right out with reasons; the rapid growth is one reason to expect that online education will continue to grow. The article goes on to give reasons why online education is superior to traditional classes: It adapts to student responses, offers flexible schedules, and is less expensive. In the comment boxes, this reader has noted that most of the evidence comes from people in the business of providing online education, so they are biased. Using the argument elements to read critically also makes it evident that the author has not considered opposing reasons, a weakness in the argument.

The notes on the GO provide the content needed to write the summary response, which is presented in the accompanying box text, "Summary-Response on Source 1 on Online Learning." Notice how it follows the elements of a summary-response paper. The first sentence makes use of one of the sentence frames to refer to the article (see Figure 5.4). Then the main reasons and key evidence are explained. The response points out that the article did not consider opposing positions and that some support is from business leaders in online education. The response ends with the student's thoughts about the ideas, which is an important step in later integrating ideas from sources with one's own ideas.

Collaborative Practice

After modeling, the next step in the Strategy for Teaching Strategies is collaborative practice. As noted earlier, the purpose is to engage students in using the strategies and to build community among students so they can learn from each other. In collaborative practice, instructors ask students to explain the strategies and their importance and then to carry out the strategies. The instructors function as facilitators, asking questions that support the navigation through the writing process. However, if students get stuck, instructors can step in with some modeling.

Please note that the collaborative work uses a second article on the same topic as the modeling. Thus, at this point in the lessons, students will have their own brainstorm on the topic and notes on two source articles. The notes on the two articles can be used in the next step of the strategy, "Integrate ideas from the sources with your own," and to work collaboratively to plan and write an essay. We will provide an example of that in Chapter 6.

Figure 5.4. Sentence Frames for Summary-Response

Summary-Response Sentence Frames (MLA)

Introductory Sentence

The first sentence should mention the title (or source) and the author, and give the overall position (or central idea) of the author. Follow MLA rules to italicize publications, use quotations for titles, and include page numbers if necessary.

- In [title* or *source*], [author's last name] argues that [position OR central idea].
- In [title* or *source*], [author's last name] explains / describes [overall topic].
- In [title* or *source*], [author's last name] discusses [*two sides of issue*].

Main Element Sentences

Subsequent sentences should present the main ideas, including reasons (or main points) and opposing reasons with rebuttals (if present). The ideas should be attributed to the author through frequent mention of the author. Some key evidence can be included:

- [Author] claims that [reason or main point].
- Another reason mentioned by [Author] is [reason or main point].
- Others disagree with [Author], claiming/arguing opposing position.
- [Author] responds by saying [rebuttal, with evidence].

Response

The response should evaluate the arguments, comment on the credibility of the author and source, and reflect on the ideas.

- The author's [claim, argument] is [OR is not] supported by specific evidence; [explain how this strengthens or weakens the argument (e.g., data, expert].
- In my view, [give your thoughts on the issue].
- One idea from the article that I might use in my own essay is [reason, evidence]; [explain how].

Signal Phrases

When summarizing an essay or article, describe the author's ideas with words such as:

- *argues, asserts, claims, demonstrates, describes, disagrees, discusses, explains, maintains, points out, proposes, reports, responds, shows, states, writes*

Peer Review

We noted in earlier chapters the importance of learning self-evaluation and the role of peer review in learning to evaluate. Peer review generally happens after students complete a draft of a paper. However, in the case of critical reading and note-taking to write a summary-response, we have found it valuable to have students compare and discuss their notes before writing the summary-response. They are asked to check whether they identified the same main ideas (e.g., reasons on both sides). If not, they check their highlighted articles and revise their notes if appropriate. Note that there is often more than one way to read a published argument, so they are not required to agree. However, the discussion gets them to reflect on their understanding and to see how a peer made use of the highlighting and note-taking strategies. Students also peer review their completed summary-response papers using the rubric.

CONNECTING SUMMARY-RESPONSE TO WRITING ESSAYS WITH SOURCES

Instructors will need to make decisions about how many summary-response papers to assign. It is certainly not necessary to write a summary-response for every source that one uses in writing an essay. The summary-response papers give students an opportunity to practice strategies for critical reading and note-taking while writing about single sources. In addition to the critical reading and note-taking, they learn how to write sentences that explain ideas from a source; they also learn how to express criticism of source ideas. It is a good idea to give them the experience of writing one or two essays using sources for which they wrote summary response papers. However, once students have had some experience, they can transition to using the critical reading and note-taking strategy and then moving directly to the integration strategy to use their notes to write an essay with sources. This is the focus of the next chapter.

CONCLUSION

> The summary response essays were very useful because students were being asked to think about the whole article, the author and source and their credibility, and then how they're going to use information from that article. And their criticisms of the article. I think that is definitely a technique that is rarely used. I never thought about putting it all together. I taught reading the content, but not all the other parts. I thought that was good because it was done in a very organized fashion.
>
> —reflection from an instructor on a post interview

This statement shared by a collaborator comments on the function and benefit of the strategy as a whole and of its subcomponents. As we shared earlier, writing using sources is a common "ask" in college. However, it is not possible for students to effectively complete without some form of systematic instruction. Strategy instruction offers them a system and structure that guides their reading attention and supports their writing skills. The organization in the process can be seen reflected in the writing of students and in the organization of their ideas as they effectively communicate with their readers.

CHAPTER 6

Integrating Ideas From Sources in an Essay

As noted in Chapter 5, writing with sources is cognitively demanding. The first challenge is comprehension and critical reading of source texts with the purpose of identifying content to use in writing. Many college students, especially students in developmental classes, have difficulties with reading comprehension, and even generally proficient readers can benefit from instruction in writing using sources. Chapter 5 focused on strategies for reading and writing summary-response papers to address this challenge. The second challenge is integrating, or synthesizing, ideas from sources and one's own knowledge to create a coherent argument that considers multiple perspectives. Such integration is challenging even for accomplished writers. It is also important for intellectual development. This chapter focuses on explaining strategies for integrating ideas from sources with your own and then planning how to present them in a well-organized essay. Objectives relevant to the goal of writing using sources can be found in Chapter 5.

SEQUENCE OF ASSIGNMENTS

Once students have written two summary-response papers on sources about one topic, they are ready to begin to focus on the next strategy: *Integrating ideas from sources with your own.* In general, for the first assignment in which students integrate sources to write an essay, we recommend using a topic and two sources for which students have already written summary-responses. In this way, students will already have a good understanding of the content and will have begun to critically evaluate the ideas in the sources. Since students will have already engaged with the sources, it is usually appropriate to start out with explanation and collaborative practice, rather than modeling, for this first essay with sources.

Next, the instructor might assign summary-response papers on a second topic followed by a second essay, but with more independence. For example, students might write summary-responses on two or three sources, then begin planning collaboratively, but write their essays independently. In this way, students can get support during the process with the challenging aspects of integrating sources in their plan.

Next, students might have a choice of topics and work independently or in groups interested in the same topic. At this point, they do not need to write the summary-response papers, just use the critical reading and note-taking strategy and move on to integrating ideas from sources, followed by planning, drafting, and revising.

In the next section, we describe the process for introducing the strategy for integration of sources, after students have written two summary-responses on a topic. We explain the instruction for integrating ideas from sources with your own in some detail and then continue with explanations about planning, drafting, and evaluating/revising for essays with sources. Completed materials to illustrate the process will be included with the explanations; the topic for these sample materials is whether educational media is good for young children.

INTRODUCTION TO WRITING USING SOURCES

It is important for students to understand that writing an essay with sources, or a research paper, involves consideration of opposing viewpoints and strategies for integrating perspectives. Without that understanding, many students will read to find information that supports their own beliefs, read uncritically, and write one-sided papers. The instructor should lead a discussion to make it clear that it is not enough to summarize what others said, nor to pick facts that support their own position. Rather, the goal is to think about ideas on both sides of an issue, look for agreements and disagreements, choose their own position, and select and organize ideas in a persuasive way. It is good to discuss some examples of when they use sources to make decisions (e.g., reading reviews to decide what cell phone to buy, or reading to decide who to vote for).

As noted previously, because students have already engaged in critical reading on the topic, it is more appropriate to use collaborative practice than modeling. Actual think-aloud modeling is difficult when much of the content is already familiar to students, and they have already taken notes on the sources. However, if students are stuck, or instructors see opportunities to expand their understanding, it is a good idea to step in with some modeling of thought processes.

INTEGRATE IDEAS FROM SOURCES WITH YOUR OWN IDEAS

Discuss the Ideas

The first step in integrating ideas is to discuss the ideas with peers. Just as they discussed their notes on individual source articles, students can now discuss their thoughts about the varied sources and what reasons they find to be the

Integrating Ideas From Sources in an Essay

strongest. This discussion can begin with small groups followed by sharing and discussion with the whole class. The purpose of these discussions is to get students started thinking about their positions and the reasons/evidence they might use. The next steps will guide them in a more organized way. The topic used in the completed examples is about whether online education is helpful for college learning. This topic was used in the example in Chapter 5.

Display Your Notes

Next, students need to display their own brainstorms from "Begin with what you know" and their notes on the GOs for the source articles. Their task is to look for connections, beginning with agreements and disagreements on positions and reasons. It is generally easiest to do this on paper copies. Students can highlight agreements and disagreements or mark them in other ways. Students should display their own materials on their desks. They can discuss them in pairs and share with the whole class the agreements and disagreements they found. Figure 6.1 shows a completed TAAPO and brainstorm from "Begin with what you know" on the topic of online learning. The student has managed to come up with a few reasons and examples on both sides. Figures 5.3 and 6.2 show completed notes on the Argument GO for two sources related to online education. The two sources present pro and con positions. The first source, which was used in Chapter 5, argued that online education is the future of education. The other source argues that online education is not nearly as effective, at least for undergraduates, as face-to-face classes.

Use the T-Chart

The same T-chart that was used in "Begin with what you know" can now be used to gather the most important ideas from the sources. Students should be reminded to keep an open mind and look for the strongest reasons. The instructor should explain that agreements offer opportunities to provide evidence from multiple sources to support a reason. On the other hand, disagreements can offer opportunities for rebuttals. Students should also include their own ideas from the initial brainstorm. It is important to keep track of sources by adding a source note of some kind (e.g., author name, date) to each entry. This part can be done collaboratively as a whole class. The instructor can display a blank T-chart, either on a computer display or large paper chart, and solicit ideas from students based on their peer discussions. Figure 6.3 shows a completed example with selected ideas on both sides.

Decide What to Say

Next, a decision must be made about which side to support in the essay. In general, we encourage students not to make up their mind until

Figure 6.1. Completed Example for "Begin With What You Know" on Topic of Online Education

TAAPO

    T (**Topic**). Is online education helpful for learning?

    A (**Author**). Me

    A (**Audience**). College students, professors

    P (**Purpose**). Persuade

    O (**Organization**). IROC, introduction with position, reasons, opposing reasons, conclusion

Idea T-Chart

Use for brainstorming.

Topic or Issue: Is online education helpful for learning?	
One Side: Yes, it's good.	**Opposing Side:** No, it's worse for learning.
It is easier for students to attend class from home. For some classes, can take class any time of day. Can show videos. Can go back later and look at class.	It's hard to pay attention. It's just not the same as seeing the professor. Why would I pay so much to take a class on TV? You can't talk with other students. Class is boring.
What questions do I have?	
Are there ways to do it better?	

they have thought about the reasons and evidence, though we recognize that more often students will know what side they agree with from the beginning. For collaborative practice though, the class will need to decide. The instructor can encourage them to take the side with the best evidence.

Integrating Ideas From Sources in an Essay

Figure 6.2. Completed Example of Notes on Source 2 on Online Education

Close Reading: Take Notes Using the Argument Graphic Organizer (GO)

Citation: Herman, P. C. (2020). *Online learning is not the future*. Inside Higher Ed. https://www.insidehighered.com/digital-learning/views/2020/06/10/online-learning-not-future-higher-education-opinion		
Issue/Problem: Is online education good for student learning?		
Author's position (or central idea): No, online education is not good for student learning because students don't like it.		
Reasons (or main points)	Key evidence (or supporting details)	Comments
Students felt like they learned less online than in a face-to-face class.	One student said she learned about 10% as much online as she did F2F. Others didn't feel school was as demanding or meaningful.	
Students felt cheated by parts of online learning.	Many students lost their jobs and regular class times, leading them to feel like they had no life and schedule anchors.	The distraction is real. I find myself doing other things on the computer during online classes.
	They were distracted by stuff at home, like siblings and pets.	My kids also distract me.
	They were also were off task during online class—social media, playing games, and shopping.	
	Paying too much money for online classes.	
Students felt isolated and missed community.	Students got videos and felt like they were alone in the class.	The personal relationships make learning more fun.
	No discussion, questions, or conversations. People learn when they work together.	

Figure 6.2. *Continued*

Opposing position (if present): Some people think online education will solve education's problems.			
Opposing Reasons	Support/Evidence	Rebuttal	Comments
The pandemic is a chance to transform education.	Hans Taparia, in a *New York Times* op ed, wrote online education could solve colleges' money problems from COVID-19. Jeb Bush and Andrew Cuomo assert that education should move past classrooms.	Herman's students don't want their education transformed.	Politicians usually know very little about the education.
Zoom, while imperfect, helps to restore some of the student-desired community.	Having regularly scheduled classes helped restore some of the scheduling anchors for students. Zoom helps people to have a discussion that's like a face-to-face classroom.	There are issues with Zoom and student privacy.	Is the camera on or off? Did none of the students have concerns about their fellow students' backgrounds?
Online teaching is good for some.	Those with physical handicaps and those impacted by COVID-19.		

PLAN YOUR ESSAY: ORGANIZE IDEAS WITH THE ARGUMENT GO

After completing the T-chart, the next step is to select and organize the ideas to use in the essay. As in writing without sources, the GO will include the issue and position, reasons with evidence, opposing reasons with evidence and rebuttals, and ideas for the conclusion. This process is done collaboratively with the whole class, with the instructor recording ideas on the Argument GO. Working collaboratively with the whole class allows the instructor to provide guidance and step in with modeling if needed. The process of making connections among ideas continues as students select and organize ideas from the T-chart and from the notes as needed. As the GO is filled out, the instructor and students should be sure to review the content to make sure that the argument is coherent. Are the issue and position clear? Are the reasons connected to the position and supported with evidence? Are the opposing reasons supported with some evidence but also rebutted effectively? Of course, these questions are the same as those on the evaluation rubric, and appropriately so. It is good to find any problems here before

Integrating Ideas From Sources in an Essay

Figure 6.3. Completed Example Integrating Ideas From Sources

Idea T-Chart

Use for integrating ideas from sources.

Topic or Issue: Is online education good for student learning?	
One Side: Yes, online education is good.	Opposing Side: No, it is harmful.
Scheduling is flexible for students. (Koksal) Good for busy professionals. Online education is less expensive. (Koksal) Software like Zoom can make online ed better. (Herman)	Regular class times help students structure work. (Herman) Distractions at home and on the computer itself. (Herman) College students during the pandemic did not like online education. (Herman) F2F discussions are important for learning.
What questions do I have?	

spending time on drafting. Figure 6.4 shows a completed GO with the ideas that the students have decided to include in their essay; note that the position taken does not reject online education entirely but states that it is not effective for undergraduate classes.

DRAFT THE ESSAY

The strategy for drafting a paper is similar to writing without sources though more complicated because it requires writing sentences to introduce source ideas. The plan on the GO provides an outline of the content, so writers can follow the plan and focus on clarity of writing and adding details. It is difficult to complete a full essay with sources through collaborative writing. However, it is important to do some drafting to show how writing with sources is different. A reasonable goal is to draft the position statement, the topic sentences for the reasons and opposing reasons/rebuttals, and one body paragraph. Drafting a body paragraph provides an opportunity to show students how to incorporate the source material into their essay using the sentence frames from the summary paper (see Figure 5.4). The main goal of this initial collaborative practice is to show students how the planning strategies work. They will have opportunities for more independent writing, peer review, and editing on a second essay with sources. Thus, it is fine if the complete essay is not written.

Figure 6.4. Completed Example Argument Graphic Organizer for Planning

Use for planning your own essay.

Issue/Problem:		
Is online education good for student learning?		
Author's position (or central idea)		
For undergraduate college students, face-to-face instruction is better than online courses.		
Reasons (or main points)	Key evidence (or supporting details)	Comments
Discussions with the professor and other students are difficult online.	In-person classes make it easy to ask questions and have interesting discussions. Students complained online classes not personal. (Herman)	
Students get distracted in online classes. (Herman)	Distractions from home environment—pets, other people, tasks. Distractions on the computer itself—email, social media, video games, even shopping.	
Opposing position (if present)			
Online education is the future of education.			
Opposing Reasons	Support/Evidence	Rebuttal	Comments
Scheduling is flexible.	Good for working professionals (Koksal) who need to learn specific skills.	But for undergrads, structured class times are important. Keep them on task to get work done.	
Less expensive. (Koksal)	Same course can be taken repeatedly with less teaching time.	True, but students are paying the same and getting less.	

FURTHER ASSIGNMENTS

Second Assignment With More Independence

On a second assignment, after students write summary-response papers on a new topic, the class could work collaboratively again to plan an essay using the "Integrate ideas from sources" strategy and the "Plan essay" strategy. Then students could draft their essays independently and bring them to class for peer review and revision. The evaluation and revision strategy is similar to the process for essays without sources. The difference is that the evaluation criteria include questions about use of sources (see Figure 2.5).

Third Assignment

Following the principle of gradual release of responsibility, students can now move on to work independently with guidance as needed. At this point, students do not need to write summary-response papers for all the sources they use. They can use the critical reading and note-taking strategy to prepare notes on the GO and use that to integrate ideas across sources. Instructors can provide a choice of topics with source articles. If appropriate for the class, students can be asked to find an additional source, or sources, on the topic; or students can be given free choice of topic and find their own sources. Of course, if students are expected to find sources, they will need instruction on how to do that using the resources available at the college.

Instructors may choose to include collaborative activities during the process. For example, students may work in small groups interested in the same topic to compare their notes on sources and engage in discussion about alternative positions on the issue. Of course, peer review of drafts will still be part of the assignment along with instructor feedback and work on editing.

SELECTING SOURCES

Using sources selected by instructors has important benefits for students who need considerable support in writing with sources. Sources can be selected with consideration of student interests and reading levels; use of common sources facilitates modeling and collaborative practice as well as peer discussions of the source articles and comparison of notes on a particular source. Instructors can see which students need more support in their reading and note-taking. On the other hand, selecting sources can take substantial time by instructors either individually or in teams.

In our work, we have generally looked for topics related to familiar social issues, including issues of local importance. For example, one of our instructors chose "smoking in public places" as a topic because the college was considering implementing a policy prohibiting smoking throughout the campus, including parking lots. It can also be a good idea to select topics with a theme. One semester in our research, we selected topics related to technology in general, including social media, online education, media for young children, self-driving cars, and increasing automation of many jobs. Reading over the course of semester on a theme can build student knowledge and familiarity with types of arguments, which helps their writing. Of course, writing in disciplinary courses always will have this thematic feature.

An important issue to consider is where to find articles. We found it relatively easy to find argumentative and discussion pieces on social issues in newspapers and magazines. It was also very easy to find unreliable, misleading information in magazines and online in general. Thus, if students are encouraged or permitted to find some sources on their own, they will need to learn how to evaluate the credibility of online sources. Another option is to limit sources to articles found through searching on databases of professional journals and respected newspapers. Then students will need to learn how to search on databases and still need instruction in evaluating credibility and bias.

Another alternative for finding sources is to use a student text with readings. Many such works are available. One of the instructors we worked with used a student text of readings on social issues from newspapers and periodicals (Atwan, 2017). It included a dozen topics, such as immigration, free speech on campus, and gender, with four to six published articles on each. The challenge for the instructor then became selecting topics and articles that would be interesting and comprehensible to the students.

One of our instructors reported that "students loved the online learning topic and articles. They have lived it and had a lot to say. The articles took strong positions on opposite sides. Interestingly, most students took positions in the middle, saying that online education had positive effects in some cases."

CONCLUSION

Learning to engage with opposing positions on an issue that students find interesting and important can be energizing. One instructor from New Mexico, with whom we worked after completion of the formal research studies, said:

> They did great with your program. They really loved it. They told me that they planned to use some of the skills from it in [another course]. I just had so many really good experiences with it.

> —interview with participating instructor

The confirmation by the instructor not only addressed the use of the program in their class but also the transfer of strategies, tasks, and skills by students from their class to other classes. Students knew they had knowledge and strategies that would be useful in other settings and were able to transfer them because they felt knowledgeable and confident. The same instructor explained that in the process of learning how to write using sources, one of the students conducted an interview and treated the interviewee as a source.

> "One of them went, at my suggestion, to one of the historians, we have a historian who specializes in the Southwestern U.S. He actually was a source for

the student's paper, and he really liked that, sitting down and talking with him, interviewing him, quoting him for the paper."

—interview with participating instructor

The student was able to reach out to the source, conduct an interview, take notes, utilize the information in their paper, and cite the source. In this case the student conducted research that involved interpersonal communication. This required confidence and the ability to express the intent of the task and of the interview. Constructing an interview also required knowledge of the purpose of the task. Thus, all the skills and strategies the student had acquired supported their ability to seek information and to cite information in written texts and also from people who had expertise and knowledge about the specific topic.

Part III

A LOOK TO THE FUTURE

CHAPTER 7

Addressing Challenges in Implementation and Problem-Solving

> If students didn't understand the reading, then it was hard for them to think through their response to it. Learning how to paraphrase when they don't understand what they read, well, obviously they couldn't paraphrase it. The thing I had to keep doing was to help them pull apart what their own thoughts were, keeping their opinionated thoughts out of the parts where they would say, "this is what the article says." Keeping their tone objective until they got to what their own thoughts were. That's fine; you can agree or disagree but you still keep it professional.
>
> —response from a collaborating teacher

This excerpt from an instructor interview reflects the challenges that one of our collaborators shared during implementation. It is anticipated—as with any instruction—that all will not go as planned; however, it is important to be aware of what components may be challenging and how best to prepare to address or anticipate them. By the end of this chapter, instructors will be able to identify ways to address challenges with the following issues:

- Instructional delivery of cognitive strategies and students' implementation
- Students' motivation
- Writing without sources
- Writing with sources

CHALLENGES WITH THE USE OF COGNITIVE STRATEGIES

Challenges with the use of the strategies for composition may not only be for students but also for instructors. Those challenges may address both the strategies themselves and their use and instructional delivery.

Challenges for Students

It is likely that students have heard of the terms *strategies* and *writing process* in their previous schooling, or the terms may have been referenced in other classes. However, it is unlikely that they have received instruction on strategies in such a systematic manner. Therefore, it is possible that there may be a slight unintentional resistance to using all the instructional components. For instance, students may skip brainstorming and move to drafting immediately. They may also skip the graphic organizer (GO) and use information from the brainstorming to draft their paper. In those instances, it is important to explain the reasoning for the completion of all those components and how they support the students as writers overall. Instead of punitively removing points from a packet they submit, make sure to ask students why they choose to skip a specific step. Such discussions with students can help the instructor to better understand (1) how to deliver information to students by better addressing the importance of a specific step and (2) how to explain to students the effects that such omission has on their writing.

During brainstorming and development of ideas, students tend to be selective of ideas to develop and include in their plan. However, at the brainstorming stage the goal is for them to generate all possible ideas. Therefore, the teacher should model the development of several ideas and then the selection of some in the completion of the graphic organizer. In brainstorming, the goal should be to come up with all possible ideas.

Challenges Shared by Instructors

Something we have heard several times across our collaboration is the challenge instructors have or concerns they share about the completion of the modeling live with think-aloud. The challenge seems to be the belief that students will be disengaged and that they will not be able to follow the instructor if they only listen to what the instructor presents, and they do not participate actively. However, it is important to understand the reasoning for the modeling. The point of think-aloud modeling is to make the cognitive processes audible and visible for students so they hear why they need to use a specific strategy and how. Explaining the strategies while working through the writing tasks is significant as this is the model students will use when they work independently. The more explicit the instructors are, the more beneficial the lesson will be for the students. Further, it is necessary for students to see the challenges, the struggle in a way, that instructors face as writers so they see that writing is a challenging task for all writers.

> *Sometimes, students feel overwhelmed because they think that their writing method is wrong (no matter what it is). They don't realize that all writers*

struggle with a lack of ideas or feeling like there's no good way to write something. Seeing the think-aloud shows them the universality of writing problems and that even experts struggle.

This comment by one of our collaborators truly showcases the powerful nature of modeling that allows students to see not only the challenges but also how to overcome them through the use of specific strategies. Thus, it is important for instructors to consider the following:

- When working on modeling, the thinking process should involve not only what strategies to use but also explaining why the strategies are important. This information will help students remember and also understand the significance of each of the strategy components and use them instead of skipping them.
- During modeling, the completion of the modeled text should be on a topic that is interesting to students. A discussion about relevant societal topics can stimulate students' interest and focus prior to modeling or collaborative writing.
- Similarly, when working on writing using sources, it would be helpful for the readings to be interesting to students so they have the desire to learn more about a topic. Otherwise, they may be disengaged. Further, students may not have the necessary background knowledge to follow the content of an article. This is why it may be helpful to first discuss topics to develop background knowledge or offer some shorter readings or videos to support background development.
- The composing of a paper during teacher modeling should be on the level of the students. Thus, the completed paper should represent the type of paper students are expected to produce. This is important to consider as instructors draft to avoid using words or phrases that may be unknown to students who, as a result, cannot follow the instructor's reasoning.
- The completion of the drafting should involve the generation of sentences of varied length and structure. The instructor should model and experiment with the development of different sentences and sentence structures. This is a way to show students how they can use language flexibly to express their ideas. Of course, the use of transition words and sentence frames can guide the sentence development.
- If the instructor runs out of time during the modeling lesson, they may stop after the completion of the graphic organizer but not after the brainstorming. That is because it is helpful for students to see how the ideas are selected from the brainstorm and placed in the graphic organizer. The next time the class meets, the teacher may continue with the modeling of drafting.

- When working on writing using sources, it is important to consider what sources to use. Instructors may predetermine the topics and offer to students a set of readings on topics of interest (e.g., climate change, educational system, increase of minimum wage) or give students the choice to select their own sources. If the latter is decided, we advise instructors to spend time modeling and practicing how to evaluate sources. This is why in the developmental courses we first suggest that sets of readings are offered so students first devote their energy into writing using sources instead of searching, evaluating, and selecting sources to read and integrate.
- In addition, it is possible that students may find the actual reading of sources challenging. This is why the strategy of summary and response can be essential for them to comprehend the reading and also to confirm their understanding after meeting and sharing with another student. It is helpful for students to work on the summary and response for the articles they use.

Metacognitive Challenges

> The strategy that I had the most trouble understanding was the goal-setting strategy. I found it a bit confusing because when asked what my goals for my writing would be, naturally I would think it's to get a passing grade. But as I learned more about the strategy, I learned that it wasn't asking me that, instead it was asking what I want others to get from my writing.
>
> —reflection from a student participant

As we discussed in Chapter 2, it is not enough to address cognitive strategies; it is equally important to address metacognitive ones. Students learn to set goals, select strategies, monitor their use, and reflect both on the use of strategies and on their performance. Addressing goals is a challenging concept for students. It is not enough to tell students to set goals and think of their goals. That is, students may not be able to think of goals. The comment shared by the student demonstrates this challenge, which is not unique to this writer. The ability to understand goals and to set goals is something that requires support to develop and time to be truly applied by students. Additionally, students might have had goals in the past that were not accomplished. As a result, they may not feel as able to complete their goals, or they may dismiss the entire process of goal setting. Therefore, instructors should explain what goals are and how the specific strategies help students accomplish those goals. For example, the completion of a self-evaluation rubric helps students identify specific revisions they need to complete for the current paper (see Chapter 4). In addition, students can use the self-evaluation to reflect on how they used the writing strategies and then set goals to use strategies in more effective ways for the next paper (see Traga Philippakos, 2019; Traga Philippakos & MacArthur, in press).

Sharing with students everyday examples of goal setting can help them better understand the meaning of goals and of alternative actions. For example, instructors may offer as an example weight loss. In the following section, we provide a sample teacher talk:

> *Let's say that my goal is to lose weight; to be exact 10 pounds. I need to do this for health reasons and because I would like to have more choices on what to wear. That is my main goal. What strategies may I select? Well, I could lower my calorie intake. I will make a plan to eat a good breakfast with cereal, eggs, juice, and fruits. I will have a late lunch and then something light for dinner. My main strategy then is calorie control. I will make a plan to use this strategy for two weeks. In order to monitor how my strategy works and whether I am accomplishing my goal, I will weigh myself at the end of each week. By the end of the second week I see I have lost one pound. I also reflect thinking that I am hungry at night and do not really sleep well. I also seem to begin to overthink the calories and lose the enjoyment of eating and tasting different foods. Therefore, I do not really think that this strategy alone is helpful. I need to keep my goal, which is to lose weight, but perhaps I should be specific. Therefore, I will say that I need to lose four pounds by the end of week two. Regarding strategies, I will eat healthy and include more fruits and vegetables, avoiding fats and saturated fats. I will have three meals a day, but I will also go to the gym three times a week and will have walks in the evening after work. I will be also weighing myself every week instead of doing that every other week. By the end of the first week, I notice that I have more energy and feel more energized. I also weigh myself and see I have lost two pounds already with this change of strategies. My goal is to continue being realistic and continue with the goal to lose two pounds every week. My goals are realistic, and my strategies are effective. Regardless, though, I will continue to reflect on the use of the strategies and modify my goal or the strategies.*

In this example, the teacher shared a simple explanation to introduce goals, strategies, the process of progress monitoring, and of reflection. After this example, the class may discuss goals students had and then gradually transition to the specific goals they have for the writing class. This will be a nice way for the teacher to discuss the *Strategy for Academic Success* (SAS; see Chapter 2) and for students to comment on their own goals.

Admittedly, it is not easy for students and adults to share challenges they may face with a large group of people they do not know. This is why in the initial classes, it would be helpful to engage students in group discussions so they get to know each other; in addition, it is important for students to have the opportunity to share their thoughts about the strategies and their use in journals. These journals can include different questions that the instructor shares for students to reflect:

- What did you learn today that you think could help you as a writer? How do you plan to use that information?
- What are your specific writing goals now that you have learned these writing strategies and the use of the IROC elements to organize your ideas?
- What are some of the challenges you still face as a writer? How can the strategies help you write papers that clearly communicate ideas to readers?

Students may also share their journal responses with their classmates individually or as a group. Students may also be encouraged and reminded to use these strategies in other classes and share the ways that these strategies were used and their effects. Such use of strategies outside of the context of the one class can help students see that they are applicable across writing contexts. However, this transition to sharing with the group or with one another should not be rushed, so students feel comfortable to share. Sharing challenges can make students vulnerable. It is essential that they feel accepted and not judged when they share. Thus, teachers should be also open in their explanations and give space for students to express their vulnerability. For example, teachers may share a specific goal they had and ways that they needed to modify it. Similarly, teachers may share their own challenges as writers and ways that they gradually improved through the implementation of specific strategies. This can help them also connect with their students and make the learning process a group's goal.

Technology Challenges

It is not uncommon for students to type their work in college; often it is an expectation. Unfortunately, even though online classes during COVID-19 required an increase in the use of typing, not all students have adequate typing skills. However, it is important that they have sufficient typing fluency to compose their work. Research shows that typing fluency affects writing quality on assessments (Connelly et al., 2007). It may be a good idea to introduce students to computer-based typing programs and make the programs available for practice.

Further, students may lack general knowledge of formatting; specifically they may not know how to format their papers or may even have trouble creating new documents. It is important that during modeling instructors demonstrate and explain some of the basics of document creation, formatting, and typing requirements. The following is a short list of some of the more basic and general; however, there are many more:

- How to create a new document
- How to name it and save it
- Where to save it and be able to find it after
- How to copy a document
- How to create paragraphs and indent
- How to change the font and font size

As students work on their own papers, they may be provided with specific reminders and "how to" sheets so they remember how to complete specific tasks. However, it is more efficient if they are shown these tips during the modeling phase and also if they practice with the teacher during collaborative practice and are given the opportunity to write and receive support by the teacher or by partners when they work on their own paper.

INSTITUTIONAL ORGANIZATIONAL STRUCTURES

Community colleges and other institutions of postsecondary education are not organized like K to 12 settings. College-level instructors usually have more autonomy regarding their instruction and the materials they use. Further, professional development is not centralized and predetermined by the institution, but each individual teacher may seek a professional conference or organization for their own learning and professional growth. Because of that level of autonomy, the implementation of this program or its PD may not be decided by central office or personnel who evaluate data and develop annual instructional goals for PD (see Traga Philippakos, 2020b; Philippakos & Voggt, 2021). If instructors are interested in this instructional approach, they may apply it in their class or collaborate with other colleagues to do so.

Chapter 8 discusses implementation options that connect with specific organizational structures (e.g., co-requisite courses). During our implementation and development, we worked with some colleges that had a central leader who worked to establish consistency across all sections of relevant writing courses, including those taught by tenured faculty, nontenured faculty, and adjunct personnel. We also worked with individual faculty at colleges who learned about our program and wanted to try it out; a trial by one instructor sometimes led to other faculty becoming interested. In other words, it is possible to implement the SSW approach on an individual basis as well as on a college or department-wide basis. The latter requires more planning and coordination, but it also opens opportunities for faculty to collaborate in adapting the approach to their setting.

END OF SEMESTER REFLECTION

After a long semester and student engagement on the use of strategies for writing and for reading, it is important to discuss with students how the strategies can be used in other courses and contexts. Some students may have already used the strategies in other classes. For example, TAAPO can easily be applied across courses. It would be helpful for students to share their experiences using the strategies in other classes and the benefits (e.g., they were better able to complete an assignment and complete it on time) and consider ways that they could expand the use of those strategies in their next classes.

> *I am taking Sociology 101 this semester and already I have had to write two short papers. After learning of the strategies, I had a good idea on how to organize my thoughts. The strategies I have learned in English 110 have helped me in other classes. I received an A for both of those papers. I had an enormous amount of detail, my instructor said. The fact that I had a lot of detail was totally due to the fact that I learned in my other writing that detail is key. I cannot wait to use the organizational elements on other papers!*

—written reflection from a student participant

The reflection shared by this student celebrates the transfer of knowledge and strategy use from their present class to other classes successfully. Such reflections and conversations can support students' confidence for use of those strategies beyond the context of the writing class. And that is the goal of this program: for writing to be meaningful and for students and teachers to apply the strategies across courses.

CONCLUSION

> "When I started this English class, I was worried because I feel like I'm not such a good writer. I feel like my writing is weak and not so interesting. But as I learned the strategies, the most helpful strategy was the writing strategy. It was the most helpful because I would just write a paper without planning or drafting and I would always get low grades on my papers. Since I started using these strategies, my writing has improved SO much and writing now is not as complicated to write papers. By using these strategies I can set goals, brainstorm, and write a strong paper."

—written reflection from a student participant

As this student response indicates, learning to use strategies that support their writing is a challenging process but also a rewarding one. The student

Addressing Challenges in Implementation and Problem-Solving

who shared information about their experience admitted difficulties with expression of ideas and the quality of their work. However, they celebrated the change in their work once they committed to using the strategies. We hope that readers of this book will read and hear similar responses from their students.

In this chapter, we shared anticipated challenges and ways to resolve them. It is important to keep in mind that the goal is not only the instruction of cognitive strategies but also the application of metacognitive ones. It is helpful for students—especially for learners who have received disappointment and criticism as writers—to see that there are strategies that can be easily implemented, that they have control of their use, and they can reflect and adjust their use from one paper to the next. In addition, it is important for students to see that writing is a process that requires time, but one that all students can learn to do; therefore, it is not a matter of ability alone, but also a matter of effort and of commitment to strategy use. Writers may not be able to complete specific tasks yet (see Traga Philippakos, 2020a), but the use of the strategies and students' continuous reflection on their use can support them in growing as confident writers who can write about what they read.

The teacher's role in this process of development is essential. The teacher is the model that students will follow both on the cognitive strategy use and on the metacognitive strategies. The ways that teachers problem-solve during modeling and the ways that teachers guide students to reflect and set goals for strategy use can affect learners' motivation and ability to select and use strategies (Traga Philippakos, 2021). Thus, when both teachers and students celebrate writing and the ideas that students share, the writing becomes a means of communication—as it should be—and not only a teaching and learning objective.

CHAPTER 8

Extending the Strategies to Other Genres and Other Courses

In Chapter 2, we explained that writing strategy instruction includes three key elements: the design of the strategies, the pedagogical methods, and metacognitive self-regulation. The strategies in SSW draw on rhetorical knowledge of genres and their purposes combined with cognitive processes for critical reading, planning, evaluating, and revising. Pedagogically, what works is clear explanation of the strategies together with think-aloud modeling and collaborative practice. Finally, metacognitive strategies are needed for self-regulation of the writing and learning process. All of these design elements can be applied to any type of writing, and writing strategy instruction can potentially be used in any course that involves writing.

This chapter will discuss applications of SSW in courses beyond developmental writing and integrated reading and writing courses, including first-year composition and courses in other content areas.

ADAPTING STRATEGIES TO GENRES ACROSS COURSES

Chapters 3 and 4 already provided examples of strategies for argumentative and compare-contrast writing. In our curriculum, we also have units of instruction on personal narratives, procedural explanations, and cause-and-effect explanations. These types of writing are quite general genres, though in one study we made the personal narrative more specific by basing it on National Public Radio's *This I Believe* series (https://www.npr.org/series/4538138/this-i-believe). There are many genres of argument. In Chapter 5, we noted that the argument essay form that students write differs from published arguments, such as an op ed piece, which may begin by refuting arguments made by others and may assume that readers have knowledge about the issue. A scientific research paper is an argument with a research hypothesis as the position and experimental evidence leading to a conclusion. A policy proposal may take the form of first arguing the importance of some problem and then arguing for a particular solution. A history paper providing an explanation of some event can also be considered an argument for a particular interpretation of the event, but with much different types of evidence than a science paper or policy proposal. Similarly, instruction in technical writing courses commonly focuses on learning about the purposes and organization of genres used in workplaces, such as business letters, memos, and proposals (Read & Michaud, 2018).

To use strategy instruction to teach writing in a genre, one needs to do a rhetorical analysis of the purpose, audience, organizational elements, and some key linguistic features. A graphic organizer, or structured outline format, can be designed with the organizational elements. An evaluation rubric, similarly, can be based on the organizational elements. Depending on the genre, sentence frames might also be helpful.

EXAMPLES OF APPLYING THE SSW STRATEGIES IN OTHER COURSES

Although our research has focused on developmental writing courses and integrated reading/writing courses, many college students, especially first-year students, could benefit from SSW in other courses that involve writing. Many of the colleges and individual instructors who worked with us on our research not only continued to use SSW in developmental education after the study, but also began to use the strategies in other courses, including FYC, co-requisite courses that combine developmental writing and FYC, summer bridge programs, first-year seminars, and upper-level courses that require writing, including history and literature.

Of the six colleges that participated in our three experimental studies, two adopted or adapted SSW for all their developmental writing courses. One of the colleges that participated in the first study (MacArthur et al., 2015) adopted SSW in 2013 and has used it ever since. They helped with the design research on adding source-based writing and adapted their own course accordingly. We helped to provide professional development until they developed their own expertise to provide PD for new faculty. They also began using the SSW strategies in FYC. Recently, in alignment with recent moves in the field to reduce developmental courses, they eliminated their upper-level developmental writing course and use SSW for FYC.

The second college that adapted SSW for developmental writing also participated in the design research to expand SSW to include writing with sources. After that design research, they continued to adapt the curriculum to their setting in innovative ways, led by Kim Donnelly (Donnelly et al., 2022; Donnelly, 2023). First, they offered integrated reading and writing (IRW) in a 7-week semester with FYC in a 7-week session in the same semester. Second, they gave students placed in developmental education a choice between three courses. The first option, "The Academic Essay," followed the SSW instructional approach. The second option, "The Academic Presentation," used strategies from SSW for critical reading and synthesizing courses, but instead of essays, students created oral presentations with slides as the final outcome. The third option focused on grammar and sentence writing, and students wrote reflective essays. More than half of students selected the first option. Overall, students who passed the IRW course and enrolled in FYC passed at rates comparable with students not placed in developmental education and without taking a full semester developmental course.

Several instructors have reported using SSW in teaching FYC. Many first-year students can benefit from learning the critical reading and writing strategies with instructor modeling and collaborative practice. Peer review is a common practice in FYC, but research shows that it is more effective if students are prepared for evaluation (MacArthur, 2016); the SSW strategy for using genre-based criteria makes the process clearer and more specific. In addition, clear criteria also make giving feedback easier for the instructor since students will know what it means when the instructor says that the opposing reason is mentioned but not rebutted well. The metacognitive strategies—goal setting, task management, progress monitoring, and reflection—can be useful in any course.

One instructor, who began working with us after the research studies had been completed, first used the SSW program in her developmental course. She learned about our program from a conference presentation and accepted our invitation to collaborate. We worked with her entirely online; in addition to online conversations and meetings, we also shared materials including a few videos. Therefore, this instructor did not have the full PD. After the first semester, she reflected:

This is a great system, and it's probably the most effective way of teaching source-based argumentative writing I've ever used. I'm so grateful. The only thing that bothers me right now is that since it's my first time teaching it, I am not doing as well as I probably could after I would if this were my second attempt, but there's a first time for everything, right?

—interview with participating instructor

In the next semester, as her college transitioned to offering co-requisite courses, she used SSW in a co-requisite course that included 10 students placed in regular FYC and 10 in developmental writing. The developmental students stayed for a second session after class, and the other students were invited to stay as well. She reported that the approach worked equally well for both groups of students.

In addition to Donnelly mentioned previously, four other instructors who participated in our early research studies and continued to collaborate with us have adapted the SSW approach to instruction in a range of courses. In Chapter 1, we mentioned Eric Nefferdorf's quasi-experimental study (2020) that used SSW in a 4-week compressed course at the start of the semester, leaving time for students to complete an 11-week FYC course in the same semester. As we noted, the study found a large effect on quality of student writing.

Three other instructors, Blake, Gallagher, and Cottle, have recently written about their application of the SSW approach in other courses (Blake et al., 2023). Michelle Blake was also first author on a journal article (Blake et al., 2016) that summarized the early research evidence and explained *why* and *how* the approach was successful in improving both student writing and motivation. We highly recommend reading the article. Blake has used the writing strategies and metacognitive strategies in FYC, in first-year experience courses, and in business writing. Elements of SSW that she consistently uses include analysis of good and weak student writing samples from previous semesters, modeling and collaborative practice with gradual release of responsibility to independent work, and most important, the metacognitive strategies for goal setting and reflection.

Caitlin Gallagher worked with us to adapt the SSW approach for a summer bridge program at our home institution, the University of Delaware. The university does not have developmental courses, but they do have summer courses for students who are accepted but need additional work on writing in preparation for college work. Students take 5-week, one-credit courses in writing and/or math along with a one-credit course on "academic self-management." Gallagher worked with us to adapt SSW for the course, planning the syllabus and setting up the materials on the learning management system. She and three other instructors, who had worked with us previously, taught sections. Overall, they reported that the critical reading and integration strategies were especially helpful. Integration is challenging and often leads to plagiarism, and the note-taking strategies reduced inadvertent copying. They thought that the strategies helped students to see argumentative writing as understanding multiple perspectives and forming their own perspectives, rather than just citing references. They also found that collaborative discussion of the articles contributed to building understanding. One challenge was that self-management strategies were taught in a separate one-credit course, which required coordination with other instructors not familiar with the SSW approach.

Katherine Cottle, the fourth of these consulting instructors, has taught a range of courses in English and the humanities and has used the SSW strategies in courses on history, literature, and a senior seminar capstone course. For example, in a history course on contemporary global issues, students read three articles from periodicals each week and write a reflection paper on one of them. Through this reading, they select a topic for their final course project. Students learn to use the critical reading and note-taking strategies from SSW and the reflection papers involve summary and response.

As noted previously, one of our consulting instructors applied SSW in a business writing course. We think that the writing strategies and metacognitive strategies in SSW would fit well in technical writing, or business or professional writing, courses, which are designed to prepare students for writing in the workplace. Technical writing courses are the second most common college writing course after FYC. A recent survey (Read & Michaud, 2018) of instructors of technical writing found that 88% teach workplace communication genres, such as memos, letters, proposals, and reports. Substantial numbers of instructors in the survey (66%) also said that they teach students how to analyze writing tasks in work contexts. FYC develops students' general writing skills but usually with a primary focus on preparing students for writing in college courses. Workplace writing differs from college writing in that the primary focus is on practical outcomes rather than learning, and it more often involves communication and collaboration with colleagues. The demands of writing in the workplace vary substantially by occupation (Handel, 2016). Thus, students need to learn specific genres and also learn how to analyze the genres they will encounter in the workplace. The importance of rhetorical analysis of audience and purpose and on learning appropriate genres fits well with the SSW approach. Future research should explore the use of SSW in technical writing courses.

CONCLUDING THOUGHTS

Our research program has provided strong evidence that strategy instruction with metacognitive self-regulation is an effective approach for developmental writing and integrated reading/writing courses. As the examples in this chapter indicate, strategy instruction also has potential application in a wide range of college courses, including writing courses and disciplinary courses. A scientific research paper is an argumentative genre with a research hypothesis as the position and experimental evidence leading to a conclusion. Papers in history also build arguments, but with much different types of evidence than a science paper or policy proposal. Following strategy instruction procedures, instructors could explain the purpose and organization of writing assignments in their courses, provide good and weak examples, and model the process of planning and writing.

The summary-response paper in SSW is related to assignments in many college courses that ask students for critical reactions to a reading task. For example, students might read a research article related to science concept in a science class, or an interpretation of a historical event in a history class, and then critique it using what they have learned in the course. For these tasks, students need to know the main elements to look for while reading and the kinds of critical questions to ask while reading. Is the article accurate and based on scientific or historical theories; are the research methods valid?

We remain interested in working with colleges and instructors who would like to explore the Supporting Strategic Writers program and discuss how it might be used and adapted to meet their needs. More information and instructional materials are available on our website: supportingstrategicwriters.org. We encourage interested colleges and instructors to contact us for more information and potential collaboration.

References

Adams, P. (2019). *The Hub: A place for reading and writing.* New York: Bedford/St. Martin's.
Applebee, A. N., & Langer, J. A. (2011). A snapshot of writing instruction in middle schools and high schools. *English Journal, 100*(6), 14–27.
Atwan, R. (2017). *America now: Short readings from recent periodicals* (12th ed.). New York: Bedford/St. Martin's.
Bailey, T., Jeong, D. W., & Cho, S. W. (2010). Referral, enrollment, and completion in developmental education sequences in community colleges. *Economics of Education Review, 29*, 255–270. https://doi.org/10.1016/j.econedurev.2009.09.002
Bandura, A. (1986). *Social foundations of thought and action: A social cognitive theory.* Hoboken, NJ: Prentice Hall.
Barnett, E. A., Kopko, E., Cullinan, D., & Belfield, C. R. (2020, October). *Who should take college-level courses? Impact findings from an evaluation of a multiple measures assessment strategy.* Center for the Analysis of Postsecondary Readiness. https://academiccommons.columbia.edu/doi/10.7916/d8-262b-wq33
Barzilai, S., Zohar, A. R., & Mor-Hagani, S. (2018). Promoting integration of multiple texts: A review of instructional approaches and practices. *Educational Psychology Review, 30*(3), 973–999. https://doi.org/10.1007/s10648-018-9436-8
Bereiter, C., & Scardamalia, M. (1987). The psychology of written composition. Hillsdale, NJ: Lawrence Erlbaum.
Blake, M. F., Cottle, K., Gallagher, C., & MacArthur, C. A. (2023). *Supporting metacognition: Effective learning strategies for the first-year student and beyond.* [manuscript submitted for publication]. Department of English, Westchester University.
Blake, M. F., MacArthur, C. A., Mrkich, S., Philippakos, Z. A., & Sancak-Marusa, I. (2016). Self-regulated strategy instruction in developmental writing courses: How to help basic writers become independent writers. *Teaching English in the Two Year College, 44*(2), 158–175.
Bureau of Labor Statistics. (2022, May). *The economics daily.* U.S. Department of Labor. https://www.bls.gov/opub/ted/2022/61-8-percent-of-recent-high-school-graduates-enrolled-in-college-in-october-2021.htm

References

Chen, X. (2016, September). *Remedial coursetaking at U.S. public 2- and 4-year institutions: Scope, experiences, and outcomes (NCES 2001–405)*. U.S. Department of Education, National Center for Education Statistics. https://eric.ed.gov/?id=ED568682

Cho, K., & MacArthur, C. (2011). Learning by reviewing. *Journal of Educational Psychology, 103*(1), 73–84.

Cho, S., Kopko, E., Jenkins, D., & Jaggars, S. S. (2012, December). *New evidence of success for community college remedial English students: Tracking the outcomes of students in the Accelerated Learning Program (ALP)*. New York, NY: Community College Research Center. https://eric.ed.gov/?id=ED538995

Connelly, V., Gee, D., & Walsh, E. (2007). A comparison of keyboarded and handwritten compositions and the relationship with transcription speed. *British Journal of Educational Psychology, 77*(2), 479–492.

Council of Writing Program Administrators. (2014). WPA outcomes statement for first-year composition (v3.0). *Journal of the Council of Writing Program Administrators, 38*(1), 144–148.

Council of Writing Program Administrators, National Council of Teachers of English & National Writing Project. (2011). *Framework for success in postsecondary writing*. Authors. https://wpacouncil.org/aws/CWPA/pt/sp/statements

Dimino, J., Gersten, R., Carnine, D., & Blake, G. (1990). Story grammar: An approach for promoting at-risk secondary students' comprehension of literature. *The Elementary School Journal, 91*(1), 97–119.

Donnelly, K. (2023). *Yes, developmental students can thrive in integrated courses and compressed terms: Leveraging institutional data and national trends to build the best reading/writing program*. Teaching and Learning Excellence through Scholarship, 3(1).

Donnelly, K., Gonzalez, J., Werner, J., Dodson, Y., & Schlueter, C. (2022, January). *Integrated reading and writing: Three flavors, two modalities, and one dramatic shift to 7-week terms*. Paper presented at the Association of Faculties for Advancement of Community College Teaching, Columbia, MD.

Edgecombe, N., Jaggars, S. S., Xu, D., & Barragan, M. (2014). *Accelerating the integrated instruction of developmental reading and writing at Chabot College*. (CCRC working paper no. 71). New York: Community College Research Center. https://academiccommons.columbia.edu/doi/10.7916/D8CZ359B

Englert, C. S., Raphael, T. E., Anderson, L. M., Anthony, H. M., & Stevens, D. D. (1991). Making writing strategies and self-talk visible: Cognitive strategy instruction in writing in regular and special education classrooms. *American Educational Research Journal, 28*(2), 337–372. https://doi.org/10.3102/00028312028002337

Flavell, J. H. (1979). Metacognition and cognitive monitoring: A new area of cognitive–developmental inquiry. *American Psychologist, 34*(10), 906–911.

References

Flippo, R. F., & Bean, T. (Eds.). (2018). *Handbook of college reading and study strategies* (3rd ed.). New York: Routledge.

Graham, S., & Harris, K. (1989). Components analysis of cognitive strategy instruction: Effects on learning disabled students' compositions and self-efficacy. *Journal of Educational Psychology, 81*(3), 353–361.

Graham, S., Harris, K., & Chambers, A. B. (2016). Evidence-based practice and writing instruction: A review of reviews. In C. MacArthur, S. Graham, & J. Fitzgerald (Eds.), *Handbook of Writing Research* (2nd ed., pp. 211–226). New York: Guilford Press.

Graham, S., Kiuhara, S., & MacKay, M. (2020). The effects of writing on learning in science, social studies, and mathematics: A meta-analysis. *Review of Educational Research, 90*(2), 179–226.

Graham, S., McKeown, D., Kiuhara, S., & Harris, K. R. (2012). A meta-analysis of writing instruction for students in the elementary grades. *Journal of Educational Psychology, 104*(4), 879–896. https://doi.org/10.1037/a0029185

Graham, S., & Perin, D. (2007). A meta-analysis of writing instruction for adolescent students. *Journal of Educational Psychology, 99*(3), 445–476.

Granado-Peinado, M., Mateos, M., Martin, E., & Cuevas, I. (2019). Teaching to write collaborative argumentative syntheses in higher education. *Reading & Writing, 32*(8), 2037–2058. https://doi.org/10.1007/s11145-019-09939-6

Handel, M. J. (2016). What do people do at work? A profile of U.S. jobs from the survey of workplace Skills, Technology, and Management Practices (STAMP). *Journal for Labor Market Research, 49,* 177–197. https://doi.org/10.1007/s12651-016-0213-1

Harris, K. R., & Graham, S. (2009). Self-regulated strategy development in writing: Premises, evolution, and the future. *British Journal of Educational Psychology Monograph Series II, 6,* 113-135. https://doi.org/10.1348/978185409x422542

Hayes, J. R. (1996). A new framework for understanding cognition and affect in writing. In C. M. Levy, & S. Ransdell (Eds.), *The Science of Writing* (pp. 1–27). Erlbaum.

Hayes, J. R., & Flower, L. (1980). Identifying the organization of writing processes. In L. W. Gregg & E. R. Steinberg (Eds.), *Cognitive processes in writing* (pp. 3–30). Erlbaum.

Hebert, M., Gillespie, A., & Graham, S. (2013). Comparing effects of different writing activities on reading comprehension: A meta-analysis. *Reading & Writing, 26*(1), 111–138. https://doi.org/10.1007/s11145-012-9386-3

Hillocks, G. (1984). What works in teaching composition: A meta-analysis of experimental treatment studies. *American Journal of Education, 93*(1), 133–170.

Hodara, M., & Jaggars, S. S. (2014). An examination of the impact of accelerating community college students' progression through developmental education. *The Journal of Higher Education, 85*(2), 246–276. https://doi.org/10.1080/00221546.2014.11777326

Koksal, I. (2020, May 2). The rise of online learning. *Forbes*. https://www.forbes.com/sites/ilkerkoksal/2020/05/02/the-rise-of-onlinelearning/?sh=1257f8a472f3

MacArthur, C. A. (2011). Strategies instruction. In K. R. Harris, S. Graham, & T. Urdan (Eds.), *Educational psychology handbook: Application to learning and teaching* (Vol. 3, pp. 379–401). American Psychological Association.

MacArthur, C. A. (2016). Instruction in evaluation and revision. In C. A. MacArthur, S. Graham, & J. Fitzgerald (Eds.), *Handbook of writing research* (2nd ed., pp. 272–287). Guilford.

MacArthur, C. A. (2023). Integrated reading and writing instruction in college. In Graham, S. & Traga Philippakos, Z. A. (Eds.), *Writing and reading connections: Bridging research and practice (pp. 311–330)*. New York: Guilford Press.

MacArthur, C. A. (2023). Postsecondary developmental education in writing: Issues and research. In X. Liu, H. Hebert, & R. A. Alves (Eds.), *The hitchhiker's guide to writing research: A festshrift for Steve Graham*. Springer Nature.

MacArthur, C. A., & Graham, S. (2016). Writing research from a cognitive perspective. In C. MacArthur, S. Graham, & J. Fitzgerald (Eds.), *Handbook of writing research* (2nd ed., pp. 24–40). Guilford.

MacArthur, C. A., & Philippakos, Z. A. (2013). Self-regulated strategy instruction in developmental writing: A design research project. *Community College Review, 41*(2), 176–195. https://doi.org/10.1177/0091552113484580

MacArthur, C. A., Philippakos, Z. A., & Graham, S. (2016). A multi-component measure of writing motivation with basic college writers. *Learning Disability Quarterly, 39*(1), 31–43. https://doi.org/10.1177/0731948715583115.

MacArthur, C. A., Philippakos, Z. A., & Ianetta, M. (2015). Self-regulated strategy instruction in college developmental writing. *Journal of Educational Psychology, 107*(3), 855–867. https://doi.org/10.1037/edu0000011

MacArthur, C. A., & Traga Philippakos, Z. A. (2022). Supporting students' writing from sources at college entry. In T. Hodges (Ed.), *Handbook of research on writing instruction for equitable and effective teaching* (pp. 338–358). IGI-Global.

MacArthur, C. A., Traga Philippakos, Z. A., May, H., & Compello, J. (2022). Strategy instruction with self-regulation in college developmental writing courses: Results from a randomized experiment. *Journal of Educational Psychology, 114*(4), 815–832. https://doi.org/10.1037/edu0000705

MacArthur, C. A., Traga Philippakos, Z., May, H., Potter, A., Van Horne, S., & Compello, J. (2023). The challenges of writing from sources in college developmental courses: Self-regulated strategy instruction. *Journal of Educational Psychology. 115*(5), 715–731. https://doi.org/10.1037/edu0000805

Mateos, M., Martín, E., Cuevas, I., Villalón, R., Martínez, I., & González-Lamas, J. (2018). Improving written argumentative synthesis by teaching the integration

References

of conflicting information from multiple sources. *Cognition and Instruction, 36*(2), 119–138. https://doi.org/10.1080/0737000,2018.1425300

Nastal-Dema, J. (2019). Beyond tradition: Fairness, placement, and success at a two-year college. *Journal of Writing Assessment, 12*(1), 1–18.

National Center for Education Statistics. (2012). *The nation's report card: Writing 2011* (NCES 2012–470). Institute of Education Sciences, U.S. Department of Education, https://nces.ed.gov/nationsreportcard/pdf/main2011/2012470.pdf

Nefferdorf, E. (2020). *Design, implementation and outcomes of a condensed curriculum for an accelerated developmental education English course.* [Unpublished doctoral dissertation]. University of Delaware.

Nussbaum, E. M., & Schraw, G. (2007). Promoting argument-counterargument integration in students' writing. *Journal of Experimental Education, 76*(1), 59–92.

Pajares, F., Johnson, M., & Usher, E. (2007). Sources of self-efficacy beliefs of elementary, middle, and high school students. *Research in the Teaching of English, 42*(1), 104–120.

Perfetti, C. A., Rouet, J. F., & Britt, M. A. (1999). Toward a theory of documents representation. In H. V. Oostendorp & S. R. Goldman (Eds.), *The construction of mental representations during reading* (pp. 71–98). Erlbaum.

Perin, D., Bork, R. H., Peverly, S. T., & Mason, L. H. (2013). A contextualized curricular supplement for developmental reading and writing. *Journal of College Reading and Learning, 43*(2), 8–38. doi:10.1080/10790195.2013.10850365

Perin, D., & Holschuh, J. P. (2019). Teaching academically underprepared postsecondary students. *Review of Research in Education, 43*(1), 363–393. https://doi.org/10.3102/0091732x18821114

Philippakos, Z. A. (2017). Giving feedback: Preparing students for peer review and self-evaluation. *The Reading Teacher, 71*(1), 13–22.

Philippakos, Z. A. (2018). Using a task analysis process for reading and writing assignments. *Reading Teacher, 72*(1), 107–114. https://doi.org/10.1002/trtr.1690

Philippakos, Z. A. (2021). Writing-reading integration. In S. Parsons & M. Vaughn (Eds.), *Principles of effective literacy instruction* (pp. 163–180). Guilford Press.

Philippakos, Z. A. (2022). Genre and text structure instruction on writing and reading. In Z. A. Philippakos & S. Graham (Eds.), *Writing and Reading Connections: Bridging Research and Practice* (pp. 100–120). Guilford Press.

Philippakos, Z. A., Howell, E., & Pellegrino, A. (Eds.). (2021). *Design-based research in education: Theory and applications.* Guilford Press.

Philippakos, Z. A., & MacArthur, C. A. (2016). The effects of giving feedback on the persuasive writing of fourth- and fifth-grade students. *Reading Research Quarterly, 51*(4), 419–433.

Philippakos, Z. A., & MacArthur, C. A. (2020). *Developing strategic, young writers through genre instruction: Resources for grades K–2*. Guilford Press.

Philippakos, Z. A., MacArthur, C. A., & Coker, D. L. (2015). *Developing strategic writers through genre instruction: Resources for grades 3–5*. Guilford Press.

Pressley, M., & Harris, K. R. (2006). Cognitive strategies instruction: From basic research to classroom instruction. In P. A. Alexander & P. H. Winne (Eds.), *Handbook of educational psychology* (2nd ed., pp. 265–286). Erlbaum.

Read, S., & Michaud, M. (2018). Hidden in plain sight: Findings from a survey on the multi-major professional writing course. *Technical Communication Quarterly, 27*(3), 227–248. https://doi.org/10.1080/10572252.2018.1479590

Richter, T., & Maier, J. (2017). Comprehension of multiple documents with conflicting information: A two-step model of validation. *Educational Psychologist, 52*(3), 148–166. https://doi.org/10.1080/00461520.2017.1322968

Rose, D. (2016). New developments in genre-based literacy pedagogy. In C. MacArthur, S. Graham, & J. Fitzgerald (Eds.), *Handbook of writing research* (3rd ed., pp. 227–242). Guilford.

Rose, M. (1989). *Lives on the boundary: The struggles and achievements of America's underprepared*. Free Press.

Santangelo, T., Harris, K., & Graham, S. (2016). Self-regulation and writing: Meta-analysis of the self-regulation processes in Zimmerman and Risemberg's model. In C. MacArthur, S. Graham, & J. Fitzgerald (Eds.), *Handbook of writing research* (2nd ed., pp. 174–193). Guilford.

Schunk, D. H., & Zimmerman, B. J. (2007). Influencing children's self-efficacy and self-regulation of reading and writing through modeling. *Reading & Writing Quarterly, 23*(1), 7–25.

Spivey, N. N. (1990). Transforming texts: Constructive processes in reading and writing. *Written Communication, 7*(2), 256–287.

Traga Philippakos, Z. (2019). Effects of strategy instruction with an emphasis on oral language and dramatization on the quality of first graders' procedural writing. *Reading & Writing Quarterly, 35*(5), 409–426. http://doi.org/10.1080/10573569.2018.1547233

Traga Philippakos, Z. A. (2020a). Developing strategic learners: Supporting self-efficacy through goal setting and reflection. *The Language and Literacy Spectrum, 30*(1), 1–24.

Traga Philippakos, Z. A. (2020b). A yearlong, professional development model on genre-based strategy instruction on writing. *The Journal of Educational Research, 113*(3), 177–190. https://doi.org/10.1080/00220671.2020.1767531

Traga Philippakos, Z. A. (2021). Think aloud modeling: Expert and coping models in writing instruction and literacy pedagogy. *The Language and Literacy Spectrum, 31*(1), 1–28. https://digitalcommons.buffalostate.edu/lls/vol31/iss1/1

Traga Philippakos, Z. A., & MacArthur, C. A. (2019). Writing strategy instruction for low-skilled postsecondary students. In D. Perin (Ed.), *Wiley handbook of adult literacy* (pp. 495–516). Wiley.

Traga Philippakos, Z. A., & MacArthur, C. A. (2021). Examination of genre-based strategy instruction in middle school English language arts and science. *The Clearinghouse, 94*(4), 151–158. https://doi.org/10.1080/00098655.2021.1894082

Traga Philippakos, Z. A., & MacArthur, C. A. (2022). Reading and writing in the genres: Developing critical thinkers, writers, and readers. In T. Hodges (Ed.), *Handbook of research on writing instruction for equitable and effective teaching* (pp. 80–103). IGI-Global.

Traga Philippakos, Z. A. & MacArthur, C. A. (in press). Use of formative assessments to promote equitable practices and support learners' and instructors' goal setting for life-long growth, for the upcoming book. In T. Hodges & K. Wright (Eds.), *The Handbook of research on assessing disciplinary writing in both research and practice* (pp. 80–103). IGI-Global. IGI-Global.

Traga Philippakos, Z. A., MacArthur, C. A., & Narvaiz, S. (2019). Middle school English language arts: Design and implementation of a unit on argument using genre-based strategy instruction. *American Reading Forum Yearbook, 40*(1), 1–29.

Traga Philippakos, Z. A., & Voggt, A. (2021). The effects of a virtual professional development model on teachers' instruction and the quality of second graders' procedural writing. *Reading and Writing: An Interdisciplinary Journal. 34*(1), 1791–1822. https://doi.org/10.1007/s11145-021-10120-1

Traga Philippakos, Z. A., Wiese, P., & Davis, A. (in press). Writing and reading connections: Giving value to both sides of the same literacy coin. *Language and Literacy Spectrum.*

van Ockenburg, L., van Weijen, D., & Rijlaarsdam, G. (2019). Learning to write synthesis texts: A review of intervention studies. *Journal of Writing Research, 10*(3), 401–428. https://doi.org/10.17239/jowr-2019.10.03.01

Vygotsky, L. S. (1978). *Mind in society*. Harvard University Press.

Wodehouse, P. G. (1922). *The clicking of Cuthbert*. Herbert Jenkins Ltd.

Wolfe, C. R. (2011). Argumentation across the curriculum. *Written Communication, 28*(2), 193–219. https://doi.org/10.1177/0741088311399236

Yeager, D. S., & Dweck, C. S. (2012). Mindsets that promote resilience: When students believe that personal characteristics can be developed. *Educational Psychologist, 47*(4), 302-314. https://doi.org/10.1080/00461520.2012.722805

Zhang, C. (2013). Effect of instruction on ESL students' synthesis writing. *Journal of Second Language Writing, 22*(1), 51-67.

Zimmerman, B., & Risemberg, R. (1997). Becoming a self-regulated writer: A social cognitive perspective. *Contemporary Educational Psychology, 22*(1), 73–101.

Index

Note '*f*' denotes figure and '*t*' denotes table in the below index

Academic success
   and strategy, 21*f*
Academic writing, 3. *See also* College writing
Adams, P., 5
Applebee, A. N., 3
Argumentative writing, 14, 46, 50, 60
   elements of, 16*f*
   planning, 16*f*, 84*f*
   sentence frames, 42*f*
Argument Graphic Organizer (GO), 18*f*, 60, 70, 82
Arguments, 7
Assignments
   second, 84
   sequence of, 77–78
   third, 85

Bailey, T., 4
Bandura, A., 23
Barnett, E. A., 4
Barzilai, S., 60
Basic writing, 5
Bean, T., 5
Belfield, C. R., 4
Bereiter, C., 31
Blake, M. F., 22, 104
Brainstorming, 46, 92
   for compare-contrast, 38*f*
   and graphic organizer, 93
   installation of surveillance cameras, 37*t*
   and TAAPO analysis, 68
   and T-chart, 14, 36–41
Britt, M. A., 59

Chambers, A. B., 61
Chen, X., 4
Cho, K., 26
Cho, S. W., 4
Cognitive strategies
   challenges, 91–97
   challenges for instructors, 92–94
   challenges for students, 92
   and metacognitive challenges, 94–96
   and technology challenges, 96–97
Collaborative writing, 25, 45–46
College expectations, 5–6
College writing, 3
Compare-contrast
   sentence frames for, 43*f*
Completed Evaluation Rubric, 54*f*
Connelly, V., 96
Cottle, K., 104
Council of Writing Program Administrators (CWPA), 5
COVID-19 pandemic, 12, 96
Critical reading, 14
   strategy, 60
Critical thinking, 5
Cuevas, I., 7
Cullinan, D., 4
CWPA. *See* Council of Writing Program Administrators (CWPA)

Design research, 7
Developmental writing, 4–5
   and Supporting Strategic Writers (SSW) program, 102
Dimino, J., 14
Dodson, Y., 102

Domain-specific strategy, 13. *See also* General strategies
Donnelly, K., 102
Draft, 41–45
Dweck, C. S., 7

Edgecombe, N., 4
Editing
 and peer review, 26
End of semester
 reflection, 98
Englert, C. S., 6, 13, 14, 50
Essay, 16
 drafting, 83–84
 planning, 82, 84
 sample good student, 62–64
Essay Evaluation Rubric, *19f*
Evaluation Rubric for Argumentative Writing, 51, 53

First-Year Composition (FYC), 4, 103–104
Flavell, J. H., 20
Flippo, R. F., 5
Flower, L., 13, 23, 31
Forbes, 71
FYC. *See* First-Year Composition (FYC)

Gallagher, C., 104
Gee, D., 96
General strategies, 13. *See also* Domain-specific strategy
Genre, 7
 introduction, 24, 50
 strong and weak examples analysis, 24–25
Gillespie, A., 59, 61
Gonzalez, J., 102
González-Lamas, J., 7
GPA. *See* Grade-Point Average (GPA)
Grade-Point Average (GPA), 4
Graham, S., 5, 6, 12, 13, 14, 21, 22, 59, 61
Granado-Peinado, M., 7
Graphic organizer (GO), 15, 67, 85, 92
 and brainstorming, 93

compare-contrast, 40*t*
installation of surveillance cameras, 39*t*
Guided practice, 46–47

Handel, M. J., 105
Harris, K. R., 6, 12, 14, 20, 61
Hayes, J. R., 13, 23, 31
Hebert, M., 59, 61
Hillocks, G., 23
Hodara, M., 4
Holschuh, J. P., 5

Ideas
 discussion, 78–79
 integrate, 78–82
 and T-Chart, 79, 83
Institutional organizational structures, 97
Instructional sequence, 24–26
Instructors
 and cognitive strategies challenges, 92–94
Integrated Reading and Writing (IRW), 102
International Reverse Osmosis Certification (IROC), 50, 96
IROC. *See* International Reverse Osmosis Certification (IROC)
IRW. *See* Integrated Reading and Writing (IRW)

Jaggars, S. S., 4
Jeong, D. W., 4
Journaling, 7

Kiuhara, S., 59
Kopko, E., 4

Langer, J. A., 3

MacArthur, C. A., 4, 6, 7–8, 12, 13, 22, 24, 26, 49, 50, 55, 59, 95, 102, 103, 104
MacKay, M., 59
Maier, J., 60
Martín, E., 7
Martínez, I., 7

Index

Metacognition, 6
 and motivation, 20–22
Metacognitive strategies, 6, 12
 challenges and cognitive strategies, 94–96
 outcomes, 61
Mateos, M., 7, 60
Michaud, M., 102, 105
Model student essay, 62
Mor-Hagani, S., 60
Motivation
 and metacognition, 20–22
Motor skills, 52
Mrkich, S., 104

NAEP. *See* National Assessment of Education Progress (NAEP)
Nastal-Dema, J., 4
National Assessment of Education Progress (NAEP), 3, 3–4
National Council of Teachers of English (NCTE), 5
National Writing Project (NWP), 5
NCTE. *See* National Council of Teachers of English (NCTE)
Nefferdorf, E., 8
Notes, display, 79
 and online education, *81f–82f*
Note-taking strategy, 14, 60, 85
Nussbaum, E. M., 7, 60
NWP. *See* National Writing Project (NWP)

Online education, *70f, 80f*
 and notes, *81f–82f*
Online learning, 68–69, 71
Organizational elements, 32

Pajares, F., 20
Pedagogical methods, 7, 13, 22–24
Peer review, 16, 50–54, 74
 and editing, 26
 explanation of reasons, 51
 preparation, 50–54
 process, 51
 reasons, 51
 reflection, 55–56
 and revision, 55
 sample paper for evaluation, 54
 student practice, 55
Perfetti, C. A., 59
Perin, D., 21, 23
Philippakos, Z. A., 6, 7, 8, 13, 24, 26, 41, 50, 104
Pressley, M., 12, 20

Quasi-experimental study, 7

Read, S., 102, 105
Reading, 85
 critical, 14
 and writing, 59
Rhetorical knowledge, 5
Richter, T., 60
Rijlaarsdam, G., 60
Risemberg, R., 6, 20
Rose, D., 13
Rose, M, 26
Rouet, J. F., 59

Sample think-aloud modeling, 41
Sancak-Marusa, I., 104
Santangelo, T., 20
SAS. *See* Strategy for Academic Success (SAS)
Scardamalia, M., 31
Schlueter, C., 102
Schraw, G., 7, 60
Schunk, D. H., 20
Scientific research paper, 101, 105
Self-evaluation, 7, 49
 strategies for, 49–50
Self-Regulated Strategy development model (SRSD), 20, 22
Self-regulation, 20
Sources, selection, 85–86
Spivey, N. N., 59
SRSD. *See* Self-Regulated Strategy development model (SRSD)
SSW. *See* Supporting Strategic Writers (SSW) program
Strategic writers
 research on, 7–8

Strategy
  for academic success, *21f*
  components, 31
  core principles of instructions, 12–13
  critical reading, 60
  domain-specific, 13
  explanation and modeling, 25, 32–45
  general, 13
  key features, 7
  metacognitive, 6
  note-taking, 60
  teaching, 24–26
  for Teaching Strategies, 31
  writing instruction, 6, 13
Strategy for Academic Success (SAS), 95
Summary writing, 5, 61
Summary-response (S-R) papers, 64
  evaluation rubric, *66f*
  explanation and modeling, 67
  sentence frames for, *73f*
  to writing essays with sources, 74–75
Supporting Strategic Writers (SSW)
    program, 49, 64, 106
  curriculum, 7–8
  developmental writing, 102
  elements of, *65f*
  examples of applying, 102–105
  project, 6–7
  reading/writing courses, 9
  writing strategies, 14–20
Surveillance cameras, 43–44
  sample completed essay, 43–44

TAAPO analysis, 14, 46, 68, 71, 98
  analyze source using, 70
  assignment, 33–34
  and brainstorming, 68, 79
  and brainstorming chart, *17f*
  Writing Prompt, 34*t*
  Writing Tasks using, 32–45
TAPFOR
  writing prompt comparing high
      school and college, 34*t*
  writing prompt surveillance
      cameras, 34*t*
Task analysis, 35
T-chart, 16, 45, 47, 60
  and brainstorming, 14, 36–41

  and ideas, 79, 83
Teaching Strategies
  metacognitive outcomes, 61–74
  strategy for, 31
Technical writing courses, 105
Technology, 52
  challenges and cognitive strategies,
    96–97
Think-aloud modeling, 23–24, 92
Traga Philippakos, Z. A., 12–13, 22,
    23, 55, 59, 95, 97, 99

U.S. Department of Education, 8
University of Delaware, 104

van Ockenburg, L., 60
van Weijen, D., 60
Villalón, R., 7
Voggt, A., 97
Vygotsky, L. S., 23

Walsh, E., 96
Werner, J., 102
Wodehouse, P. G., 23
Wolfe, C. R., 59
Writing
  analyzing assignment, 35
  argumentative, 14
  basic, 5
  collaborative, 45–46
  Prompt 3.1, 33
  Prompt 3.2, 35
  and reading courses, 9
  strategy instruction, 6
  summary, 5, 61
  Supporting Strategic Writers (SSW)
      strategies, 60–61
  synthesis, 59
  using reading, 59
  using sources, 78
Writing strategies, 13–20, *15f*, 49
  research, 20

Yeager, D. S., 7

Zhang, C., 7
Zimmerman, B. J., 6, 20
Zohar, A. R., 60

About the Authors

Charles A. MacArthur, is professor emeritus in the School of Education at the University of Delaware. Major research interests include writing development and instruction, literacy, development of self-regulated strategies, and motivation with a focus on students who need extra support to be successful, including students with learning disabilities, college basic writers, and adult learners. He has directed 10 federally funded research projects on writing instruction, including two projects over the past 10 years focused on the development and evaluation of the Supporting Strategic Writers (SSW) approach described in this book. In addition, he is co-developer with Zoi Traga Philippakos of the *Developing Strategic Writers (DSW)* curriculum (grades K to 8) and coauthor with her of two books on that curriculum. Currently, he is consultant on an adult literacy project that is adapting the SSW approach for adult learners. He was coeditor of the *Journal of Writing Research* and the *Journal of Special Education*. He has published over 125 articles and book chapters and coedited or written several books, including the *Handbook of Writing Research*, *Best Practices in Writing Instruction*, and *Adult Education Literacy Instruction: A Review of the Research*. In 2020, he was named an AERA Fellow. In 2022, he received the Special Education Research Award from the Council for Exceptional Education (CEC) and the Jeannette Fleischner Career Leadership Award from the Division of Learning Disabilities. He can be reached at charles.macarthur@gmail.com.

Zoi Philippakos, Ph.D., is associate professor at the College of Education, Health, and Human Sciences at the University of Tennessee, Knoxville. Her research interests include writing and reading instruction in K to 12 classrooms and postsecondary, strategy instruction, self-regulation, and teacher professional development. Currently, she directs a project to develop and evaluate resources that address morphological analysis, writing and reading, and meaning making. Her awards include the Early Career Achievement Award by the Literacy Research Association (LRA), the Faculty Research Excellence Award from the CEHHS at UTK, and the Chancellor's Honors and Academic Award on Professional Promise in Research and Creative Achievement. She is the codeveloper of the Developing Strategic Writers

(K to 8) and the Supporting Strategic Writers (postsecondary) programs. Her most recent coauthored books are *Developing Strategic Young Writers Through Genre Instructor: Resources for Grades K to 2*; *Developing Strategic Writers Through Genre Instruction: Resources for Grades 3 to 5*; *Differentiated Literacy Instruction in Grades 4 and 5: Strategies and Resources*, and the coedited books *Writing-Reading Connections: Bridging Research and Practice* and *Design Based Research in Education: Theory and Applications*. She has published articles in leading journals (e.g., *Reading and Writing, Reading Research Quarterly*) and has presented her research and findings in national and international conferences. She can be reached at zphilipp@utk.edu and be followed on Twitter @ZoiPhilippakos.